D0978858

"You will find many wonderful things between the covers of this book: provocative questions and astute observations about sacred space, hierarchy, authority. Scattered throughout are fascinating history lessons—who knew that a musical decision made in a Seattle church in 1956 is still reverberating in early-twenty-first-century house churches? Finally, Tickle's insights will help the church reflect on a larger question: *How can we best serve the kingdom of God right now?*"

Lauren F. Winner, author of *Mudhouse Sabbath* and *Still: Notes on a Mid-Faith Crisis*

"Phyllis Tickle is in a unique position by reason of experience, education, and personal courage to say things that many cannot say—or cannot see. Here she does it very well—once again. Christianity is emerging with or without Phyllis Tickle, but she is sure helping the rest of us to emerge along with it!"

Fr. Richard Rohr, OFM, Center for Action and Contemplation, Albuquerque, New Mexico

"Finally someone has put the emergence conversation in the wider historical context it deserves—showing how what is now emerging owes so much to contributors over the last century, from Walter Raushenbusch to Johann Baptist Metz, from Dorothy Day to Mary and Gordon Cosby, from Azusa Street to Taizé and Iona to Buenos Aires. Phyllis Tickle gets it right and conveys it beautifully, so more and more readers can be a part of it . . . with a clearer understanding of what 'it' is!"

Brian D. McLaren, author/speaker/networker

"What a fascinating read! Phyllis Tickle tackles Emergence Christianity once again. In this volume, she takes the conversation further, filling in all the details and answering the who, what, where, why, and how of the movement. A page turner, I read through each story with anticipation as I eagerly awaited the next set of connections Phyllis Tickle would make between seemingly unrelated people, movements, faith, and culture. Never in one volume have I seen such a diverse set of Christian movements not only listed but analyzed for their meaning as it related to the bigger picture. Decade by decade, she walks us through the twentieth century, tracing the roots of Emergence Christianity. No one gets left behind here: we read about Pentecostalism, house churches, Taizé, Vatican II, liberation theology, Orthodox spirituality, the Vineyard, to name a few. She brings her analysis all the way up to the present day, describing the current movements of Emergence, such as Emergent Village, Neo-monasticism, New Calvinism, and others. Throughout her work, Tickle helps make a vast amount of stories intelligible, and she seems to do it effortlessly. As we have come to expect, Tickle has done her homework, and the result is a unique contribution to the conversation about what Christianity has and will become in the twenty-first century."

Dr. Ryan Bolger, PhD, associate professor, Church in Contemporary Culture, Fuller Theological Seminary

"Take a heart practiced in faith and trust in God. Add the mind of a finely trained historian and the eye of a keen observer of religion. Add gifted writing, unfailing bluntness, and deep wisdom, and you get Phyllis Tickle. These pages offer you nothing less than the future of the church, chronicled by an author who welcomes this 'great emergence' without an ounce of fear. It's a story you can't afford to miss."

Philip Clayton, dean, Claremont School of Theology

"The communities of Emergence Christianity form an often confusing and tangled mess of theology, culture, and technology. Phyllis steps into all of this with a keen and discerning eye that is part art critic, part historian, and part local bartender. In her latest book she lifts up the beautiful and the hopeful. She teaches with expert authority and a clear, simple style, all while serving up an eclectic mix of the most fascinating people, communities, and practices of twenty-first-century Christianity."

Neal Locke, 1st Presbyterian Church of Second Life

"The elegance of Phyllis Tickle's writing provides beautiful context for the comprehensiveness of her analysis: she has a bird's-eye view of what's happening to, in, and through a new kind of Christianity. . . . *Emergence Christianity* lets us into a secret that could do with being shouted from rooftops: we are all one, we need each other, and no matter the stream of Christianity you happen to feel most distance from, there's a gift waiting to be revealed when human beings open themselves to change. If you want to know how the old and the new fit together, look no further."

Gareth Higgins, executive director, Wild Goose Festival

"Are you experiencing church-death anxiety? Do you have shortness of breath when thinking about the decline of Christianity in America? Phyllis is your healer. Sit. Take a deep breath. And read."

Rev. Nadia Bolz-Weber, founding pastor, House for All Sinners and Saints, Denver, Colorado

Emergence Christianity

EMERGENCE CHRISTIANITY

What It Is, Where It Is Going, and Why It Matters

PHYLLIS TICKLE

BakerBooks
a division of Baker Publishing Group
Grand Rapids, Michigan

Published by Baker Books
a division of Baker Publishing Group
P.O. Box 6287, Grand Rapids, MI 49516-6287
www.bakerbooks.com

Printed in the United States of America

Library of Congress Cataloging-in-Publication Data

Tickle, Phyllis.
Emergence Christianity : what it is, where it is going, and why it matters / Phyllis Tickle.
p. cm.
Includes bibliographical references (p.) and index.
ISBN 978-0-8010-1355-3 (cloth)
1. Christianity—21st century. 2. Church history—21st century. 3. Emerging church movement. 4. Postmodernism—Religious aspects—Christianity. I. Title.
BR121.3.T53 2012
270.8′3—dc23 2012005335

12 13 14 15 16 17 18 7 6 5 4 3 2 1

The old has gone, the new has come! All this is from God.

2 Corinthians 5:17–18 NIV

Contents

Preface

This is now the fourth time I have spoken in book form about what is happening to us as North American Christians in the twenty-first century. The first of those four volumes was written in 1994, in the early days of my tenure as religion editor for *Publishers Weekly*, the trade journal for the English-language book industry. *Re-Discovering the Sacred: Spirituality in America* was written not as a general book but as a professional one, thus its rather ponderous title. That is, it was intended as a report of sorts to publishers, booksellers, and librarians about why religion books were suddenly and abruptly—or so it seemed to most of them—riding the country's bestsellers lists and outpacing every other category and genre in both public attention and growth of market share.

The fact that what began as a professional paper or report to a professional audience became a general-audience seller spoke volumes about our American desire in the last decade of the last century to know more about what was happening in religion and why. In response to that burgeoning need, but still interpreting things through the lens of book sales and book trends, in 1996 I wrote the manuscript for what was to be published for the general reader as *God-Talk in America*. This second volume probably had as great an impact on me as it did on anyone, a circumstance that is not unusual for writers and their writings, I might add.

To say the least, *God-Talk* and the response to it helped convince me that the time had come for me to take my eye away from its narrow focus on the book industry and train it instead to look, forever after apparently, at the broad, varied, and truly wondrous larger landscape of religion as it was being lived out in America right here and right now. It was time for me to take what my profession had given me and grow it into a bank of information of more public and hopefully far broader utility.

As a result, I began to spend more of my days and weeks traveling the country, talking to audiences—both lay and clerical—learning from them, and listening as much as I was talking. Even more of my time, however, was probably spent in reading what scholars—also both lay and clerical—had said over the centuries, not to mention over the very recent past, about patterns in religion, about ecclesiology and theology, about the sociology of religion and the courses of Judeo-Christian history and its place in the land masses and political units it had formed and been formed by. The result of all of that was a third volume, *The Great Emergence: How Christianity Is Changing and Why*, published in 2008.

Now, after almost two decades since I first began this line of study, the time has come to file yet another report—not a final report in any sense of that word, but merely an interim one. Whatever else one may say of Emergence Christianity, one must also say that it is growing and shifting and reconfiguring itself in such a prodigious way as to still defy any final assessments or absolute pronouncements. What is needed in such a set of circumstances is, at best, no more than a dispatch from the field, an opportunity for us all to assess where we are, project where we probably are going, and enter prayerfully into this new thing that God is doing.

To that end, it seems to me that we would be well served at this moment to remember the words of Rowan Williams, the Archbishop of Canterbury. In counseling his flock worldwide, Williams has said repeatedly over the last few years that we are not to read and study and discuss Emergence Christianity in order that we might save the Anglican Church or any other such institution. Rather, he says, we are called to read and study and discuss Emergence Christianity in order that we may discern how best to serve the kingdom of God in whatever form God is presenting it. While most of us will indeed have to substitute "Baptist Convention" or "United Methodist Church" or "Presbyterian Church" or "Assemblies of God" or some such other term for the archbishop's one of "Anglican Church," we still can find in his admonition, I think, the attitude with which to begin a new level of investigation and conversation. Pray God that is so.

Part 1

An Interim Report

Telling the Story So Far

1

Back to Now

How Semi-Millennial Tsunamis of Change Shape Religion and Culture

Every five hundred years, give or take a decade or two, Western culture, along with those parts of the world that have been colonized or colonialized by it, goes through a time of enormous upheaval, a time in which essentially every part of it is reconfigured.[1] From the perspective of the twenty-first century, and thus from our own place in Western history, it is fairly easy for us to see that pattern writ large over the last two millennia.

Most of us have little or no difficulty in going back five hundred years in our understanding of the Christianized Western story and seeing the Great Reformation staring back at us. We can see, from the latter years of the fourteenth century to the dramatic one of 1517 when Luther posted his Ninety-Five Theses on the door in Wittenberg, the process of wrenching, deconstructing, liberating, anxiety-producing, world-rending change as it works its way, straight as the proverbial arrow, from one regimen for ordering life to a new and unprecedented one.

And everything did change. Protestant Christians tend to think of that harsh period of the fifteenth and sixteenth centuries chauvinistically, choosing to celebrate it, from the comfort of our five-hundred-year remove, primarily as a major event in the history of our faith, as a time when a new stream of Christianity was born, when old ways of doing God's business were purged, when ordinary Christians' souls were freed from human institutions and human mediation between God and the believer.

All of those things did indeed happen. It is only our mono-focus that is in error. Falling into the trap, because it pleases our religious pride or needs, of equating that fifteenth- and sixteenth-century tsunami solely with religion and of perceiving its consequences solely as matters of doctrine and religious practice is not only historically wrong but also dangerous. More to the point, it is especially dangerous for folk like us who are removed from that time of rigorous change by the fated number of five hundred years.

The Great Reformation

In point of fact—and we know this because we are taught it in school—the Great Reformation was about the change, politically, in Western governance from fiefdoms, baronies, and hereditary domains to the nation-state configuration that for most of the last five centuries has informed the Western way of ordering life. The Great Reformation was about the rise of the merchant class in accommodation to the fact that vast improvements in transportation, and thereby in commercial shipping and ordinary travel by individuals, made the merchant life not only possible but enormously profitable. The ultimate result of that, among others, was the rise and growth and, eventually, dominance of the middle class in Western culture's social order.

The Great Reformation, economically, was about birthing a new way of ordering the Western economic order; it was about birthing and then enabling capitalism as a dominant characteristic of Western ways as we have inherited them. The Great Reformation was also about a world that, in order to communicate its new ways and profit from them, abruptly needed a literate population for commercial reasons, or at the very least for several citizens in any given village or hamlet to be able to read. And no culture can go from illiteracy to increasing general literacy without shock waves.

The Great Reformation was also concerned with the discoveries being made about the physical universe and, as a result, of human ability to begin to pierce, penetrate, understand, manipulate, and even in some ways change or harness that power for "the betterment of humankind," to use an old tried-and-true cliché about it. As a result, there was a growing sense that all things—as in "every thing"—could be reduced to component parts and, once reduced, be understood.

The Great Reformation was about a whole shopping list of things, every one of them part and parcel of who we are and what our society for the last five centuries has been. Yet only a very few of those changes have to do just with religion as such. It is an important point, and one we need to be very clear about before we wander away from it.

Religion, whether we like it or not, is intimately tied to the culture in which it exists. One can argue—with only varying degrees of success, though—that private faith can exist independent of its cultural surround. When, however, two or three faith-filled believers come together, a religion—possibly more of a nascent or proto-religion—is formed. Once formed, it can never be separated entirely from its context.

Just as surely as one of the functions of religion is to inform, counsel, and temper the society in which it exists, just so surely is every religion informed and colored by its hosting society. Even a religion's very articulation of itself takes on the cadences, metaphors, and delivery systems of the culture that it is in the business of informing. Thus, when we look at these semi-millennial tsunamis of ours, we as Christians must be mindful of the fact that the religious changes effected during each of them were only one part of what was being effected, and that all the other contemporaneous political, social, intellectual, and economic changes were intimately entwined with the changes in religion and religious thought.

With that in mind, we can look back not just five hundred years to the Great Reformation but a thousand years, instead, to the Great Schism of the eleventh century when the Western world spent a contentious and bloody century and a half getting ready for the severance of East from West politically, militarily, economically, culturally, linguistically, intellectually, and—of course—religiously. As a result of the aggregate of all these confluent events, East and West would become alien to one another—natural antagonists, in fact—and Europe would get its Middle Ages in return for its trouble. Not inconsequentially, Catholicism would emerge out of the scarred remains of latinized and monastic Christianity to become the Roman Catholicism against which Luther was destined to rebel.

The Great Transformation

We can, in fact (hopefully without becoming tedious), look back fifteen hundred years from our current place in history to the Great Decline and Fall of the Roman Empire and watch as the Roman Empire crumbles into something less than even a shadow of its former self. We can watch as all communication and trade systems collapse; as formal learning ceases to be the norm for citizens; as medicine, math, and science fail; as the wisdom of the ancients is lost; and the West slides, silent as a sinking stone, into its Dark Ages. But in our watching, we will observe as well how Monastic Christianity begins to emerge as the form and organ of the faith, as the repository in aggregate of Christian treasures, the definer of its praxis, and the delivery system of its pastoral functions, of clerical training, and even of literacy itself.

We can look back from where we stand to the era of two thousand years ago when the shift was so overwhelming, so total, so cataclysmic that we know it as the Great Transformation. We continue to honor it to this day by notating the whole course of human time in the westernized world as having pivoted in just that place from "before the common era" to the "common era." We should note, by the way, that this is the era that gave us Christianity in the first place, as it emerged up out of Judaism to inform everything about us in the West, whether we are religious believers or not.

All of that is a rather absorbing story when looked at in the abstract as the delineation of a pattern or cycling in our way of doing things in Western or latinized cultures.[2] It can even be a bit enjoyable just to look back and see how the centuries have flowed. The old folk-saying that "Everything that goes around comes around" rests gently in our memories, in fact, right up until that moment when it dawns on us that the Great Reformation was five hundred years ago, the last expression of a pattern that Western culture seems fated to reenact every . . .

Mercy! That's now!

It is also us.

NOTES

1. The recurring use on these pages of the terms *West*, *westernized*, and *latinized* can become grating unless one understands the imperative for their repetition. The word *latinized* refers to those cultures and parts of the world that received their Christianity through the Latin language or were colonized by those who had so received or were colonialized by them. The other principal vehicles for the transmittal of Christianity were the Greek and the Syriac languages, both of which flourished in, and helped to create, distinctly different contexts and sociopolitical structures. There is currently little evidence that these parts of the globe and the cultures that inhabit them are susceptible to an analogous pattern of five-hundred-year upheavals. If we are to appreciate accurately what is happening in the world at large as we pass through the Great Emergence, we need to be cognizant of these distinctions.

Second, it is entirely likely that within the twenty-first century itself, the most formative change of them all for Christianity in the West will be the demographic shift in its worldwide center. In 1900, 80 percent of Christians were resident in Europe and North America. If scholarly and informed predictions and trends hold, by the middle of the twenty-first century, 80 percent of Christians will *not* be residents of either Europe or North America. Korean scholar Soong-Chan Rah of North Park University calls this shifting "probably the most significant development in church history in the past 500 years" ("Heroic Tales from Distant Lands," *Christianity Today*, April 2010, 65). Most observers either agree with Professor Soong-Chan Rah or are loath to challenge him. Certainly within the Roman communion, there is already more than enough evidence of the geographic shifting to persuade any thinking person of its impact.

As a case in point, we should note that when, in the spring of 2010, the Vatican released its annual statistical yearbook, it sent shock waves through much of the latinized Christian community. As reported by Religion News Service, this 2010 survey showed that the number of Catholics in Europe had increased by just over 1 percent in 2009. That's all well and good, of course. The arresting data, however, were that within the same time period, Roman Catholicism had grown just over 33 percent in Africa and roughly 15.5 percent in Asia. Among other things, the Vatican noted that the result of such a shift in growth patterns was that, as of 2010, only one-quarter of Roman Catholics were European. If nothing else, the implications for the election of the next pope are as enormous as they almost assuredly will be historic.

2. The whole business of cycles and cycling has so complex an academic and scholarly history as to almost defy imagination. So too does the somewhat newer field of Systems Theory. Both are far too intricate and controversial to be engaged in these pages. I have, however, been interrupted at least three or four times in or after public lectures by systems theorists who were intent, albeit not rudely, on supplying my audience and/or me with the precise and mathematical or sociological reasons for the cycles involved in any discussion of the Great Emergence. Curious or interested readers, therefore, may wish to pursue these areas in great detail and would be well served by making at least a cursory and preliminary digression into the work of general theorists like Edward Cheung, Peter Turchin, or even the most colorful of them all, the renowned Russian patriot Pitirim Sorokin, who founded the department of sociology at Harvard in 1930.

2

Calling It What It Is

The Difficulty of Naming

However one may feel about cycles and their inevitability, there is no question about the hard fact that something dramatic and irresistible is happening to every part of our lives right now, that it has been first building and then occurring for some several decades, that it became irrefutably obvious and present at a popular or lay level somewhere around or in conjunction with the opening events of this century, and that we can either be its passive medium or its active architects.[1]

Being an active architect, for most of us, is a much more appealing as well as more honorable role than is passivity. Certainly, it requires a great deal of thought and more informed consultation than does passivity, but it also requires—to use another bit of folk wisdom—that we first name the beast before we try to engage it.

Descriptive or Poetic?

A number of names have been proposed over the last five or six decades for what this upheaval of ours is. In the mid-twentieth century Carl Bridenbaugh was not only an established scholar but also, because of his influential standing in the scholarly community, held the prestigious position of president of the American Historical Society. Among other things, that office gave him a podium of authority from which to analyze the times within which he lived and to name the parts thereof. Accordingly, on December 29, 1962, in his annual President's Address to the society, speaking at the Waldorf-Astoria in New York City, Professor Bridenbaugh first discussed the cataclysmic shift that was obviously happening around both him and his community of his fellow historians, and then, after doing so, proposed that the phenomenon be named "the Great Mutation."

As a name, the Great Mutation is certainly more colorful and considerably more threatening than is that of the Great Emergence, which we use today. It is also considerably less poetic and euphonious. The surprising thing, then, at least from the perspective of half a century later, is that Bridenbaugh's Great Mutation held on to the scholarly—and to some extent to the popular—imagination for several decades. One can, in fact, still find it mentioned from time to time even today.[2]

Over the years since Professor Bridenbaugh's attempt at leaving us with the Great Mutation, various and sundry other names have been suggested, some of them even enjoying a fair amount of life in our general conversation. There have been soft and appealing terms like "a hinge of history." There is at least one bestselling book as well as a number of popular theorists arguing adamantly that our time in history is "the Fifth Turning," a titling that tips its hat immediately to the fact that, by any name, we at 2000+ CE are living dead center in the fifth such event in history.

There has been some sustained argument for using the term "the Great Convergence," which, by the way, is sometimes seen as a sequel of "the Great Divergence." I rather like the convergence one for two reasons. First, it retains "the Great" part that has been assigned to our previous mid-millennial experiences; and second, *convergence* is a very descriptive word that, unlike *emergence*, carries no freight beyond itself—a point that matters, as we will soon see.

In all of this, there is no question, however, that for me the happiest term to be suggested for naming our beast is that of Episcopal bishop Mark Dyer, who has argued since the early 1990s that we should just call the whole thing "A Giant Rummage Sale" and be done with it.

The Great Emergence Emerges

Yet despite all the colorfulness of these alternative labels, the one we hear most often and that now seems destined to stick is that of "the Great Emergence." So be it. But the minute we acquiesce to a naming, the question then becomes one of "So what is it that we have named?" In this case, the answer to that one is "Quite a lot!"[3]

Like its cycling predecessors, the Great Emergence is an across-the-board and still-accelerating shift in every single part and parcel of our lives as members in good standing of twenty-first-century Western or westernized civilization. Intellectually, politically, economically, culturally, sociologically, religiously, psychologically—every part of us and of how we are and how we live has, to some greater or lesser degree, been reconfiguring over the last century and a half, and those changes are now becoming a genuine maelstrom around us.

Most of us don't really need to be told we are living in strange and strained times, nor do we really need much cataloging of the strangenesses that assault us on a daily basis in order to accept the fact that they are there. But sometimes it is just plain fun as well as a lift of the spirits to look at some of the more bizarre or less immediately obvious presentations of this "Great Emergence" of ours. For example, I find it somewhere between amusing and distressing to know that we now have five times as many words in the English language as William Shakespeare had when he wrote his plays. We have them because, like it or not, we have five times as many things, ideas, and events to name as he had. The downside of that, of course, is that because of the Great Emergence and as part of it, technical information is now doubling at a rate of once every ten or so months, meaning that unless something slows down soon, our grandchildren will have at least five times as many English words as we have, assuming they don't die first of the overload.

It's a fact that in 1900 there were only eight thousand cars in the whole United States, but it's a result of the Great Emergence that presently there are more cars than that in an average urban neighborhood, all of them heavily involved in five o'clock traffic on any given day of the workweek. That congestion, by the way, is also a direct result, as well as evidence, of the Great Emergence.

It is the Great Emergence that the smallest of nation-states or tribal confederations can hold the largest of nation-states hostage to their own ambitions and internal strife; but it's also true that that very change allows brilliant and respected analysts like Thomas Friedman to report to us with a straight face that the world has gone flat again and then have us delight in his image. The same kind of playfulness allows the economic analyst for CNN and *Time*, Fareed Zakarias, to invent the word *mergonomics* in an attempt to defang the worldwide financial crisis that is a factor of the Great Emergence. But perhaps the most beguiling of them all is the bon mot of the Canadian scholar and bestselling author Richard Florida, who just says we should call the whole economic part of this thing "the Great Reset" and be done with it, a fiscal attitude not unlike Bishop Dyer's ecclesial one.

It is the Great Emergence—and this one is probably my favorite amongst them all—it is the Great Emergence that we are so far removed from the source of our foodstuffs that a jar of cashews at Sam's Club nowadays has to show on its small-type contents label,

"Cashew from Brazil, India, and Vietnam, Packaged in China, Manufactured by Nut Farms in Australia P/L. Please dispose of empty packaging thoughtfully." I know this, because I am the one who bought the cashews for a family party and, for the first time in my life, enjoyed the label more than the nuts.

One of the half-funny absurdities of the Great Emergence frequently repeated these days is the fact that one person or even one group of people can no longer produce so simple a thing as a lead pencil. Indeed, it now takes a truly mind-blowing conglomeration of us to produce a Dixon Ticonderoga No. 2, or at least according to George F. Will it does. He, famously now, drew public attention to that disconcerting fact in 2008 with his oft-quoted and much-cited *Newsweek* essay, "Pencils and Politics—Who Commands the Millions of People Involved in Making a Pencil? Who Is in Charge? Who Is the Pencil Czar?"[4]

Will was not exaggerating or engaging in hyperbole just for his own amusement, of course, even though he certainly made his point and had his jollies with the whole thing. Nor, I assume, was his concern really about pencils and their manufacture. It was—and at the serious level remains—about our twenty-first-century severance from the production of our simplest needs, about the growing and universal interdependence of all of us on all of us if any of us is to thrive, and about the kind of insouciance we have developed in order to avoid having to engage the obvious.

It is also somewhere between funny and pathetic that, for better or worse, we now send each other over 247 billion emails every single day. Such connectedness boggles the mind . . . or it does if one is inclined toward thinking about it for long.

It's worth noting as well that, thanks to the Great Emergence and as part of living in it, we Americans download well over ten billion iTunes songs a year now, in contrast to absolutely none in 2000. The intriguing factor in that shift is not so much the acceleration in our technological expertise or our increasing Net use or even the exponential growth in our online hours per se. Rather, the intriguing thing to consider is the obvious fact that someone has to be listening to all those tunes. And now think about that one not just in terms of hours expended or as an opportunity to employ the relatively new Great Emergence skill of multitasking; think of it also as a greatly enhanced means of human melding, and think as well of the unifying effect, semantically and emotionally, that a broadly shared aesthetic can exercise. Is this a good thing? The jury is probably still out on that one.

It is also almost a source of levity that, thanks to the Great Emergence of which it is a natural child, Wikipedia is certifiably at least 6 percent more accurate than are our most respected print-copy encyclopedias. Whatever would your grandfather make of that! It's also true, and probably even more telling, that over the first decade of this Great Emergence century of ours, we in the United States lost almost two hundred of our daily newspapers, and, Grandfather might say, with them lost almost two hundred sources of particularized opinion and perception just by losing the syndicated comics and the local daily cartoons . . .

. . . and the jests and slightly cynical observations can run endlessly on.[5] Certainly they can help to soften some very sobering insights, at least for a while. But eventually the truth behind the jests is still the truth: We are in a time of transition, and that transition is not a casual or passing one. Rather, it is yet another of the semi-millennial upheavals that have shaped latinized culture and latinized religion from their inception. We are citizens living within the Great Emergence, and as Christians of whatever stripe, we are watching the formation of a new presentation of the faith. We are attending upon the birth and early growth of Emergence Christianity.

NOTES

1. As we have already suggested, there is a period—generally of about 150 years—that leads up to each of our semi-millennial upheavals. Known as the

peri-Decline, the peri-Schism, the peri-Reformation, etc., these peri-'s or periods of buildup are like those of a pot being heated on a stove. There comes that dramatic moment when the pot's contents go from hot to boiling.

That moment of transition, in matters of Western history, if not of boiling pots, is usually the date assigned after the fact as the moment when the upheaval can be named. Thus, October 31, 1517, is routinely listed as the beginning of the Great Reformation. It is not. It is simply the date when there was no longer any way to deny that the world was in re-formation. In the same way, we are told that history will date our own upheaval from September 11, 2001, not because that was or is a pivotal North American event, which it obviously was, but because it was and remains a global one that arose from, and is evidence of, the cataclysmic shifts we now name as the Great Emergence.

The line of argument describing, explaining, and greatly illuminating the process involved here is known as *panarchy*, and it too has come up out of Systems Theory (cf. n. 2, chap. 1). I am indebted to Brian McLaren for many, many things in this life, not the least of which is his having sent me to the work in this area of men like Professor C. S. Holling, L. H. Gunderson, G. D. Peterson, etc. A Google search for "panarchy" will offer up a veritable wealth of material and external sources about a subject that, while it is somewhat tangential to our immediate concerns here, is still a major behind-the-scenes agency and a gratifying source of information for those who wish to go deeper into the causes and machinations of our current amazement.

2. We tend to forget—our kind has always tended to forget—that we live firmly embraced within the long arms of history. Our times are never ours alone. They are merely the continuation of, or sequel to, the times that belonged to our predecessors. Normally, such naïve forgetfulness does not matter greatly in the general scheme of things. In something as dramatic and laden as our semi-millennial shifts, however, forgetfulness is not a virtue. It obscures the vision and therefore beclouds with ignorance how we approach and fashion the future. It is beyond imperative, then, that we look at the struggles, however antique they may now seem to us, of credentialed, earlier thinkers like Bridenbaugh. They wrestled with that which they saw through a glass darkly but which we now see face-to-face, and the records of their earlier engagements can, if nothing else, often steer us away from repeating their missteps, misinterpretations, and miscalculations. Bridenbaugh was nobody's fool; he simply was one of the first predictive historians to talk so publicly about what he was seeing.

3. It is a bit of a reassurance in all of this to remember that our prior upheavals have all had variant names also. My favorite example of this is the fact that as recently as 2009, noted scholar and much-admired author Karen Armstrong suggested that the Great Reformation should really be called the Great Western Transformation (*The Case for God*, Alfred A. Knopf, 166). Nor was she speaking in jest.

Likewise, Armstrong offers Renaissance Christianity as a name for the five hundred years from the Great Schism to the Great Western Transformation. Beyond that, she suggests as well that the new body of Christianity coming out of the Great Reformation should be called Reformation Christianity instead of Protestantism, presumably in much the same way and for many of the same reasons that Emergence Christianity is increasingly the name being assigned to what's happening across all Christian faith-lines within our own time.

4. For a firsthand read of this rollicking and insightful essay, *see* Will's "The Last Word," *Newsweek*, September 22, 2008, 80.

5. There are dozens, if not hundreds, of facts and factoids like these now circulating through every media outlet known to exist. This particular set or shopping list draws heavily from the "Did You Know?—Rome Conference, 2008" film clip and from the delicious "Back Story" in *Newsweek*, July 26, 2010, 56, entitled, appropriately enough, "Exactly How Much Are the Times A-Changing?"

3

Defining Emergence

Simplifying the Complexity

Before we completely lay aside the Great Emergence in general and begin our consideration of Emergence Christianity in particular, we need to look—rather closely, in fact—at the word that the two of them hold in common. We need to look at *emergence* itself, and we most surely need to look with corrective concern at the innocence with which some of us tend to bandy it about. That is, *emergence* is such a well-worn word that its very familiarity often obscures to our detriment its subtleties and especially its place in the history of contemporary science.

The commonsense notion that sometimes disparate things will, for whatever reason, come together to compose a new entity is hardly unfamiliar to most of us. Nor is it news that the resulting entity usually is greater than the sum of its parts. But sometimes, and far less frequently, the resulting entity is one that not only is much greater than the sum of its parts but also one that could not have logically been predicted from a prior analysis of any single one of its parts. In that case, and among other things, the resulting entity always constitutes a major lurch forward in complexity.

Emergence Theory

When, in 1859, Charles Darwin published *The Origin of Species* and then later, in 1871, *The Descent of Man*, not all his contemporaries and peers were persuaded that his theories adequately explained all of what was happening. In particular, an early psychologist, G. H. Lewes, joined with many of his fellow scientists in holding that human consciousness was far too complex to be explained away so easily as Darwinian evolution might suggest. The exchanges were heated and, as is often true among theorists, sometimes barbed and bitter. Over the years from 1874 through 1879, Lewes published a multivolume work, *Problems of Life and Mind*, in which he argued for what he labeled "qualitative novelty." By that term, he meant to name dramatic, unforeseeable changes that cannot be entirely described or defined quantitatively, changes the results of which Lewes called "emergents." Thus began the story of what we now know as Emergence Theory.[1]

In time, Emergence Theory would give rise to a discrete body of scientific study and, in the twentieth century, would become a significant part of the growing science of Systems Theory. As our understanding of Emergence Theory expanded, so too did our ability to understand dozens of the phenomena in the natural world whose machinations and origins had previously been closed to us: things like how starfish survive the amputation of their parts even as they can grow new arms while those amputated parts can grow new and perfectly complete starfish, or how birds can fly in flocks and formations without an appointed pilot bird or centralized direction, or how anthills work and how they differ from beehives, though both have queens. The list goes on and on, but each of them is an example of Emergence, and all of them share certain characteristics.[2]

Always there is the central hallmark of complexity whose advent is (or was) sudden, unprecedented, and inexplicable. Always there is a communal element, for never is there a hierarchy. Authority or leadership is not from the top down but rather from the bottom up, or from the component parts in network with one another, and/or very often just plain sideways. In either case, horizontal instead of vertical is the direction of activity, and always—always!—what becomes its resultant structural complexity is greater than what could have been logically predicted from the structure and substance of the composing parts.

Thus, for example, who would have ever thought that, only a hundred years or so after Field Theory was physically understood and described by Faraday in 1843, a binary system of electrified zeros and ones could trigger a globalized world with all its ramifications and complexity, its instantaneous connectedness, its exponentially expanding technology, its disruptive changes in human social organization, its merged economies and economic vulnerabilities? Nobody.

Yet anybody with a modicum of history and/or of contemporary science under his or her belt would have known that, once such an upheaval had begun, there would be no stopping the evolutionary lurch forward in human complexity, not to mention in every accompanying part of human life, especially its moral, spiritual, emotional, and religious parts, which get us, obviously, to Emergence Christianity.[3]

NOTES

1. While our focus here may be only passingly on the hard-core science of Emergence Theory, it would be irresponsible, as well as inaccurate, to simply tip our hats at it without suggesting that, at the very least, a cursory search on Google would be well worth any reader's time. Literally thousands of entries about Emergence will show up there, many of them with hefty bibliographies of their own

for further investigation. Additionally, at a lay level, writers and popular theorists like Peter Drucker or Otto Scharmer, Margaret Wheatley and Deborah Frieze, etc., have employed Emergence Theory and/or Systems Theory in their economic and sociological analyses over the years. Their work is often quite familiar, as well as very accessible, to many readers and should be thought of here.

2. In the annotated bibliography included in this volume (cf. pp. 211–29), the curious will find the titles of two or three of the more popular/lay-audience volumes dealing with these very phenomena. Quite beyond those books in illuminating fun, though, is the fact that E. O. Wilson, probably our century's best-known and most respected biologist, has written an endearing as well as engaging novella about the anthill part of this whole thing. The opening sentences set the tone: "The Trailhead Queen was dead. At first, there was no overt sign that her long life was ending. . . ." For an excerpt or précis of the larger work, see "Trailhead," *The New Yorker*, January 25, 2010, or also available online at http://www.newyorker.com/fiction/features/2010/01/25/100125fi_fiction_wilson.

3. It also gets us to Emergence Judaism, which is a very similar and related story, just not the one we're focusing on here. Nor are we focusing on Emergence Islam, but it likewise exists in this country, as does a small segment of the American Buddhist community that names itself as Emergent Buddhism.

In any event, the curious may want to google "Synagogue 3000" for a ready example of what we are talking about in North American Judaism, or try "Punk-Torah" for a fairly jazzy and offbeat look at such things. The more studious reader may be better served, however, by visiting such links as http://www.forward.com/articles/135483, where he or she will find a sobering and detailed discussion of the effects of Emergence Judaism upon Conservative Judaism in North America, as well as links to related articles and observations on the same subject. And for those who lean toward a lengthier and perhaps more nuanced introduction to this area of Emergence religion in America, there could be no better choice than Dana Evan Kaplan's *Contemporary American Judaism: Transformation and Renewal* (Columbia University Press, 2011).

4

Turns of the Century

What Formed the Great Emergence?

At some point or other during the peri-Emergence time of its birthing, our present era was given the sobriquet of "the Great Emergence." Presumably that naming happened originally because, to the eyes of sociologists, professional scientists, and informed observers, our cultural upheaval was evidencing all the hallmarks and characteristics of Emergence Theory as it had been shown to exist in the physical world. The label, while it may have originated in jest or simply in the shorthand of professional conversations, has stayed on to become what it is now: the name by which we call ourselves. Oddly enough, though, during the middle and latter half of the nineteenth century, when Western or westernized Christianity first began to evidence the changes that accommodated to, or were reflective of, the secular shifts happening around it, no sociologist or trained religionist seems to have thought to tie the shifts in religion and the shifts in secularism together by assigning them a name in common.

By the closing decade of the nineteenth century and the opening ones of the twentieth, however, there was no question but that, whatever else was happening in the world at large, a whole new form of Christianity was also most assuredly being born.[1] A new expression of the Christian faith was emerging.

There have been many fine books, essays, blogs, and lectures over the last few years about the Great Emergence and its history, and there is little need for us to visit them again here.[2] Rather, if we want to more fully engage Emergence Christianity, we must narrow our focus. Moving from the more general intellectual, political, economic, and cultural history of the peri-Emergence, we must instead look selectively at some of the currents and events in ecclesial and theological history that were formative of Emergence Christianity over the century and a half of its coming. In order to do that in any useful way, however, we need to look at that word *selectively* and be quite clear, before we begin, about what exactly is and is not meant by it.

Focusing the Discussion

First, the emphasis or focus of the pages that follow is on North America and Emergence Christianity in the context of our life experience, especially in the United States. That does not mean, however, that we will restrict ourselves to North American events solely. Emergence Christianity is international in scope. Inevitably there have been and are formative exchanges across old political and cultural borders. More to the point, because we in the United States came into the Emergence conversation well after other parts of the world were deeply engaged in it, our experience has been shaped, at least to some extent, by conversations prior to our own, especially by some of those which occurred in Europe and the United Kingdom. Given that fact, to look at Emergence Christianity in total isolation would be, if not counterproductive, then at best limiting.

Second, in the next few chapters, we are going to be using a biological metaphor while looking at something that comes nearer to a prenatal and neonatal history than it does to anything else. That is, if we are to understand and engage Emergence Christianity today and predictively in terms of the near future, then the useful records for us will be those that reveal the events, circumstances, and situations that most shaped this new being while it was still in formation. What can we see in the youngster that we can better understand by looking at its prenatal or perinatal life becomes the question that will sustain us.

A Push Coming to a Shove in Catholicism

As a general rule, the first substantive evidence that a serious change is in process is the presence of organized, albeit not always well-rationalized, resistance or, put another way and just for the sake of maintaining our biological metaphor one last time, some push-back and acting out by older siblings who have begun to suspect that a new member of the family is on the way. That certainly was the case in the early years of the peri-Emergence itself. Arguably, the first real resistance to a nascent and still unnamed, unparsed Emergence Christianity was the convening in 1868 by Pope Pius IX of Vatican I. That convocation was, at least technically, seated and operative until October of 1962, when Pope John XXII officially adjourned it in order to allow for the convoking of what was to become Vatican II. Yet in all that time—in fairness, most of it was interrupted by political unrest and wars—the only real action taken by Vatican I was the establishment of papal infallibility.

Turning the pope's temporal power from a culturally and religiously accepted modus operandi into an outright formalized dogma was a kind of throwing down of the gauntlet. In the years immediately preceding 1868, the disestablishment of slavery had delivered a major blow to the principle of biblical inerrancy and, thereby, to Scripture's role as the absolute basis of authority in latinized Christendom. While the Bible does not require that one person own another, it clearly acknowledges that practice and clearly provides for its just application. And by 1868, there could be no question about the fact that abolition, whatever else it did, had declared that what was permitted in Holy Writ was wrong—egregiously wrong.[3]

The first blow had been struck. Rome had been here once before, and overall the whole thing had not been a good experience. She had no desire to be blindsided again. Better to put the fortifications and battlements in place now, at the first salvo, than to do so later when all had been lost. Thus Vatican I and thus the doctrine of papal infallibility: when His Holiness speaks ex cathedra or, that is, from the chair of Peter itself, he speaks as God's voice and cannot, as a result, speak error. The near to ironic thing in all of this, though, is that North American Protestantism, apparently innocent of any awareness that a pattern had come into play, was not far behind.

Protestants Push Back Too

The Niagara Bible Conferences met from 1878 until 1895. Technically speaking, the gatherings were called "Believers' Meeting for Bible Study" and did not even move their meeting place permanently to Niagara-on-the-Lake in Ontario until 1883. Nonetheless, the name stuck, and its consequences were to be more or less beyond measure. Like their Roman Catholic confreres, the Believers (or Committee of Biblical Conservatives, as they are sometimes called) saw the handwriting on the wall and did not like it one bit more than the pope did. Unlike their Roman brothers and sisters, however, the Committee lacked a pope to empower. Instead, they sought to empower as dogma the now seriously threatened principle of biblical inerrancy as it had come to be defined by Protestantism over the preceding two centuries. In doing so, the Believers listed five principles or theses of the faith that were nonnegotiable: the inspiration of the Bible by the Holy Spirit and, as a result, its absolute inerrancy as factual reportage; the historicity of the virgin birth; the doctrine of the crucifixion and death of Jesus as the atonement of sin; the physical and attestable reality of the bodily resurrection; and the historicity of the recorded miracles of Jesus.

These five became the fundamentals of the faith and were so named early on. Their naming also stuck at a popular level, and our words *fundamentalist* and *fundamentalism* were born into a whole new life. Equally true is the fact that the fundamentalists had, by whatever means, put their fingers right on the very places where the Great Emergence would probe traditional, or institutional, Christianity most rigorously.[4] They had named as well the doctrines of evangelicalism and/or established Protestantism that Emergence Christianity would have to wrestle with most intensely and prayerfully over the decades ahead.

We must remember, however, that Emergence Theory recognizes another fact. It recognizes that sharp changes leading to increasing levels of complexity are marked not only by resistance but also by the moving into place of unexpected, unpredicted, entirely unforeseeable things that will become components of the new thing that is being born. As the nineteenth century turned into the twentieth, that is exactly what happened. We call it Azusa Street.

What Happened on Azusa Street?

In October of 1900, a man named Charles Parham opened a small and short-lived religion school in Topeka, Kansas. Known by the rather unimpressive name of Bethel Bible College, Parham's school was destined to be the earliest breeding ground for experiences that would change Christianity forever. Looked at through the long lens of history, one can also see in Parham himself some of the proclivities and prejudices that would later inform and shape Emergence Christian thinking, especially about the nature and role of the clergy.

Though he began conducting religious meetings when he was still a teenager, Parham was never ordained. He refused to be, as a matter of fact, because he regarded it as a limitation of sorts upon the pastoral spirit. And though he attended college for a while, he left after two years, having become convinced that too much formal education also would deter him—and all other God-fearing men, for that matter—from being effective, open-to-the-Spirit preachers and pastors. Ordained or no, though, Parham did try working for a time as a supply pastor for the Methodist Episcopal Church. He soon left that as well, simply because he had serious problems with the idea of ecclesial hierarchy and especially with the notion of denominations. In general, he contended, denominational structures were such that it was impossible for a man to preach by direct inspiration as opposed to having to preach God's holy Word from within the restrictions and confines of tutored, established, and dogmatized preconceptions.

Despite his unorthodox ways, Parham was far from being a stupid man and equally far from being an arrogant one. Rather, he was a man who marched to a different and, as it turns out, very God-drenched rhythm. He had traveled widely enough to be conversant with what was then called the holiness movement and with pastors who were of persuasions similar to his own. Bethel College was born, in fact, out of his desire to gather together a community of the similarly persuaded who would pray together, seek God together, and study the Bible—and only the Bible—together. Thus it was that Bethel was also the place where, on January 1, 1901, those gathered students first began to speak in tongues. Proto-Pentecostalism had been born.

Bethel didn't last long, but Parham now knew that speaking in tongues was once more an active part of the Christian experience, that the days of apostolic Christianity had returned to the faith, and that the Holy Spirit was ready once more to be actively and visibly present among communing believers. Burning with this awareness and the experiential presence of it, Parham moved to Missouri, then Kansas, and finally Houston, where he opened another Bible school and where a young African-American man named William Seymour stopped for a while on his way West—stopped, listened, and was persuaded, for it was Seymour who was to bring to fruition the consummation that Parham had first seen glimpses of at Bethel.

The story of Seymour and Azusa Street is so well known by now that it requires little repeating. Suffice it to say that by April 1906, William Seymour had taken an old livery stable on Azusa Street in Los Angeles, reconsecrated it as a Christian meeting place, and begun to preach his belief that now was the time of the Holy Spirit. Now was the time when the gifts and charisms of the Holy Spirit were ready to be poured out on all those who would believe. Now was the time of repentance and joy and healing—and it was.

The Spirit fell upon the gathered at Azusa Street. There were miraculous healings. There were tongues of fire descending upon them. There was speaking in tongues both known and unknown. Pentecostalism had been born at last, and fully formed, so to speak.[5]

Those first Pentecostals would worship in their converted livery stable until 1915, but they most certainly would not be contained by it. Within a matter of only a few months, word of the miracle on Azusa had begun to spread across the country. Within only a few more months, the believers themselves began to spread across first the country, and then the world. Within less than a century, Pentecostalism would become the fastest-growing and the second- or third-largest body within global Christianity.[6] It would do more than that, though. It would be the natal faith and Christian experience of about a quarter of the men and women who, by the close of the twentieth century, would be Emergence Christians. Their presence early in the mix of what became Emergence Christianity was to be of inestimable import because their ready familiarity and comfort with the Spirit would feed and hone much of the core theology and praxis of Emergence itself.

The Social Gospel

In addition to Azusa Street, with its historic engagement of the Spirit and its disconcerting use of non-seminary-trained leadership, there were also some traditionally trained and established religionists who were becoming more vocal about the shifting sands of the time and about the pressing need for change within both Roman Catholicism and denominational Protestantism. Among the most articulate of these was a scholarly preacher named Walter Rauschenbusch, who for some years served Second Baptist Church in Hell's Kitchen in New York and who, as a result, knew from on-the-ground experience what he was talking about.

In 1907 and only months after the coming of the Spirit at Azusa Street, Rauschenbusch released a volume entitled *Christianity and the Social Crisis in the 21st Century*. As a pastor as well as a theorist and respected thinker, he was deeply concerned about the social and cultural implications of the young century's dramatically changing ways. The book that, in its first two or three dozen pages, speaks over and over again of "re-formation" in terms of its presence and of the need for it, was both an analysis of what was happening and, principally, a clarion call to the church to deal with it as Jesus would have dealt, had He been physically present among us.

Social Crisis is generally regarded now as the first of several foundational documents upon which the theology of social justice within Emergence thought, the Social Gospel of twentieth-century Protestantism, and the rationale of the more secular and political Civil Rights movement were all built. Certainly, it, along with Rauschenbusch's later work, was a major influence on the thinking, postures, and careers of both Martin Luther King Jr. and

Bishop Desmond Tutu, by their own admission. So seminal was the book, in fact, that its publisher, Harper, reissued it in 2008 in a centennial edition and, in doing so, heralded it as "The Classic That Woke Up the Church."

But less than a decade after Rauschenbusch's salvo, and for almost four decades following it, war as it had never before been known or experienced burst across Europe and ultimately across the Americas and the world. As tensions grew and spread during those almost forty years of warring, so too did a growling restiveness and gnawing disenchantment with the status quo, especially among ordinary latinized Christians. Even before the Second World War finally ravaged Europe, three or four things in particular were afoot. Some of them appeared to be contradictory at first, and some even quotidian or inconsequential, but in sum, they would become hallmarks of the religion forming in the midst of Rauschenbusch's reformation.

NOTES

1. Marcus Borg, a keen observer of all things religious, was among the first contemporary American scholars to affirm this at a popular or general-audience level. In his 2003 bestseller, *The Heart of Christianity* (HarperOne), Borg wrote, "The emerging paradigm has been visible for well over a hundred years." But he also went on to take note of something else of considerable, perhaps even equal, importance. He noted that "in the last twenty or thirty years, it has become a major grassroots movement among both laity and clergy" (p. 6). The significance of Borg's second observation is that it speaks to the failure of many twenty-first-century Christians to grasp the scope of what is happening simply because they have a truncated awareness of its century-and-a-half evolution as a monumental shift.

2. I have made my own contributions, for better or for worse, to this broader conversation in *The Great Emergence: How Christianity Is Changing and Why* (Baker, 2008).

3. Several things want saying here, more as reminders than as necessary parts of the larger story being told in the body of this particular chapter. The first is that Luther and his fellow reformers, once they had disestablished the pope, the curia, and the magisterium as the source of authority, had had to look elsewhere for some new seat of authority. In doing so, they turned to Holy Writ, establishing it as the source from which all authority was now to flow. In crying *sola scriptura, scriptura sola*, they more or less inadvertently laid the foundation for what was, over

the subsequent centuries, to morph into the doctrine of "Protestant Inerrancy." It is this doctrine that the fundamentals were based on and that the fundamentalists were, and still are, defending.

For many Christians—especially Protestant ones—one of the most difficult and/or frightening parts of attempting to understand Emergence postures and theology has to do with trying to believe that it is possible to be both Scripture-based and Bible-believing while, at the same time, decrying Protestant Inerrancy. We will address that conundrum a bit later in our discussion of Emergence theology as such.

4. The implication here may seem to be that Niagara was the only response to changing times, and nothing could be farther from the truth of the thing. The focus of the present volume limits, of necessity, the range of what can legitimately be presented here. Even so, it still is imperative that we recognize, if only in passing, that the whole of the nineteenth century in North America was one seething cauldron of religious unrest and discontent. The nineteenth century saw, in this country, the birthing of Mormonism, of Seventh Day Adventism, of Jehovah's Witnesses, of Christian Science, of New Thought and Unity, and of Unitarian Universalism, not to mention the coming of Theosophy. The Restoration Movement, under the Campbells and Barton Stone, spawned the Disciples of Christ, the Church of Christ, and the Christian Church in this country, and the Evangelical Christian Church in Canada. In addition, there was a resurgence of membership in Methodism over the whole continent and among Baptist bodies.

5. The romanticist in me can never make mention of Azusa Street and its miracle without also making note of the fact that once again it was in a stable in which it all began.

6. The indecisiveness here is due to the fact that different statisticians assign differing positions to the business of ranking by size. All agree that Pentecostalism is the fastest-growing segment of worldwide Christianity. Likewise, all agree that Roman Catholicism is the world's largest communion within Christianity. The difference of opinion is whether Protestantism or Pentecostalism is the second-largest Christian communion worldwide. The amusing thing in all of this is that by the time demographers arrive at some resolution to the quandary, Emergence Christianity may well have trumped both of those two contenders.

Part 2

A Long Time Coming

How Did We Get Here?

5

House Churches

Communities of Change

It was between the two great world wars that European Christians first began to evidence documentable movement away from attendance at, or involvement with, established church in whatever form it appeared. Concomitantly and somewhat paradoxically, however, there was the beginning of the first quiet, unpretentious, under-the-radar return to the so-called house church form of worship that had been the norm for the early church of the first and second centuries. In Belgium and parts of France, in particular, that shift back to house-church practice was enabled, or at least sanctioned, by the Franciscans. Certainly, by the mid to late 1930s, house-church worship had become so substantial that the Roman Church not only had to acknowledge its presence but also had to recognize it as an acceptable mode of worship upon occasion, albeit rarely.

But even more predictive than that, perhaps, were the almost idiosyncratic beginnings of three site-based, but global and pledged, communities that eventually would change the face of latinized

Christianity. The first of these had its beginnings in 1932 in the Bowery of New York City where a distinctly idiosyncratic dissident named Dorothy Day met an inspired and devout French curmudgeon named Peter Maurin. It was a marriage of souls and intellects, if not of flesh.

The Catholic Worker Movement

Together they would conceive of a new world in which the poor were cared for, class was a recognized abomination, and souls would be saved to glorify God here and now. In May of the next year, 1933, the two would produce the first issue of *The Catholic Worker*. Out of that inauspicious beginning would come first the Catholic Worker Movement and, in short order, the first of the Houses of Hospitality, over two hundred of which are now scattered across the globe.

Day's vision of a world made holy by radical faith, radical obedience, and radical Christian practice would become the earliest expression on a massive and popular level of the vision that, over time, would come to characterize Emergence Christianity in general. Likewise, Maurin's constant litany of "The way to reach the man on the street is to meet the man on the street" would find physical expression in those Houses of Hospitality and, as a thesis, would begin to worm its way into Emergence Christian praxis.

At almost the same time that Day and Maurin were challenging and reconfiguring institutionalized Christian thinking about the role and care of the poor in North America, a Church of Scotland pastor, George MacLeod, was laying the groundwork to address the same concern in his part of the world. Pastor MacLeod's concept was, originally at least, a fairly clear-cut and simple one: he would take a group of his fellow Church of Scotland ministers and a group of working-class men to the ancient town of Iona for the ostensible purpose of rebuilding the Abbey of Iona that had long lain ruined and moldering there. By putting pastors and working-class men together on a shared and common project, MacLeod was, of course, doing more or less exactly the same thing that Maurin was advocating in America: The way to reach the man on the street is to meet the man on the street.

Iona Community

But as with the Catholic Worker Houses of Hospitality, so too with Iona. What began as a small but very intentional work toward radical discipleship grew and morphed and then grew again. The Iona restoration group became the Iona Community. And long before the century's end, that community would have become what it is today: an ecumenical, inter- and nondenominational group of vowed Christians who, spread across the whole world, take Iona as their spiritual home or center and, in so doing, pledge themselves to Christ and to issues of peace and justice. Iona as a site would become a place of pilgrimage for thousands of other Christians who travel there seeking physical connection with the historic faith as well as with its holy practice in the twenty-first century. Both as a site and as a way of being, Iona would also become a well of living water for Emergence Christianity.

Taizé

In 1940, only eight years after Dorothy Day and Peter Maurin's meeting and only two years after MacLeod's leading the first cadre of ministers and workers to Iona, a man named Roger Schutz bought a sizable portion of land in Saône-et-Loire in Burgundy. At war's end, that land would become Taizé. And with that third, momentous act, Emergence Christianity may arguably be said to be officially off and running. It will not turn back. In fact, it won't even look back. Before we follow that trajectory, however, we should remind ourselves one more time of two things.

American Fables

The first of the two is that, in typical Yankee fashion, we in this country do indeed tend to think of Emergence Christianity as somehow being a phenomenon of our own invention and/or native to our land mass.[1] In point of fact, with the exception of a few innovators like Dorothy Day and her work, we North Americans are the Johnny-come-latelies in much of this. The usually proffered reason for our tardiness of perception and even, to some extent, for our delay in popular or widespread engagement of Emergence is that in the late nineteenth and twentieth centuries we as a country were more deeply and universally tied to "church" as a societal modus operandi and to Church itself than were other parts of the latinized world. As a justification for past misconceptions, this one is undoubtedly as sound as any, but it should never be taken as an excuse or justification for our continuing along that path of error.

The second fond fable for us as Americans is the lay notion that Emergence Christianity is more or less limited to us and that we are engaging it in some kind of proprietary isolation. The truth of the matter—and it is one we shall return to several times—is that Emergence Christianity is as global and ubiquitous as latinized Christianity is, primarily because it is a child of latinized Christianity.[2]

Both of these misunderstandings on our part, while they may at first seem to be more interesting than threatening, nonetheless can (and in some places, have already begun to) alienate us from many Emergence Christians outside the United States. More seriously, perhaps, our persistence in clinging to them can often block United States Emergence Christians and United States Emergence observers from recognizing the truly global scope of movement. It is, then, only with all of this in mind that we can return in good conscience and with open hearts to the story of Emergence Christianity in the decades since Brother Roger so providentially bought the land in Burgundy that is now Taizé.

NOTES

1. Not all North Americans have been so chauvinistic, of course. In fact, some of our fellow citizens have been more than passingly impatient with the rest of us. One of the best examples of blogosphere disgust that I have ever read, in fact, was posted in 2005 by Alan Creech, a Catho-mergent graphic designer from Kentucky, on Next-Wave (http://www.the-next-wave.info/archives/issue85/index-51900.cfm.html). The essay posted there, "What I am and what I am not—or a short history and explanation of the wider 'emerging church,'" has become a bit of a classic, its thesis caught dead-on in Creech's words: "You've got to understand that many of us have been doing what we're doing, in some form, for much longer than the term emerging church has even existed."

2. Anyone who is interested in pursuing this can begin by googling groups like *La Red del Camino*, *generacion emergente*, or *amahoro*, but one of the most promising prospects in all of this is a book under the title *Gospel after Christendom: New Voices, New Cultures, New Expressions*, edited by Ryan K. Bolger (Baker Academic, 2012).

A collection of essays from Emergence practitioners and leaders from around the latinized world, *Gospel* will provide us with an intentional and comprehensive book-length overview of global Emergence Christianity. The compilation is the work of Professor Ryan Bolger of Fuller Seminary, who both shaped the book from its conception and has served as its editor, which should not be a surprise. It was Bolger and his senior colleague at Fuller, Professor Eddie Gibbs, who, in 2005, published *Emerging Churches: Creating Christian Community in Postmodern Cultures* (Baker Academic). At that time, *Emerging Churches* was one of the two book-length overviews of Emergence available from scholars who were not themselves involved in Emergence in some way. It still stands as a sound introduction to Emergence practice both in this country and elsewhere.

6

Scattered Communities

Spreading the Word by Spreading Out

Taizé and the Ancient Disciplines

Taizé, once it had become functional shortly after the Second World War, was to evidence almost every major or defining characteristic of Emergence Christianity. From the beginning, it was ecumenical across all the communion lines of historic Christianity. It was global almost before the rest of the latinized world understood what that term really meant, much less what it was destined to mean within a matter of no more than another five or six decades. Taizé was monastic or, as an Emergence Christian today would say, Neo-monastic.

In every part of itself and its workings, Taizé was, and is, deeply and fundamentally communal. Peace and justice were, from the outset, major foci, as was hospitality in the fullest and most catholic of ways. Taizé praxis is aesthetic in orientation, and that aestheticism is first, incarnational; second, meditative; and third, unifying. That means, among other things and principally, that Taizé understood from its earliest beginnings the centrality of music to spiritual experience and how music could lift that experience up and away from the particularities of formalized religion.

Life at Taizé likewise depends from, and seeks to be deeply connected to, the ancient disciplines of historic Judeo-Christian tradition. It recognizes the sacred meal or Eucharist and the praying of the daily offices as central to Christian formation. Even beyond these, it honors and enables, as do few other holy sites, the spiritual and religion exercise of pilgrimage. Annually, over a million Christians now make pilgrimage to worship there, many of them Emergence Christians for whom Taizé, like Iona, is the mother lode, the refreshing source, whose nourishment is to be received gratefully and shared broadly.

But even as Taizé was moving from a mere land purchase in France to a fully inhabited reality, several other evidences of proto-Emergence were also occurring. Two of them in particular require mention here, and both, auspiciously enough, occurred in 1943.

Inspired by the Divine Spirit

On September 30, 1943, Pope Pius XII released to the church a revolutionary encyclical entitled *Divinio Afflante Spiritu* or "Inspired by the Divine Spirit." The choice of this date for *Divinio*'s release was not a casual one. Rather, it had great gravitas as a choice. September 30 is the feast day of St. Jerome, and it was St. Jerome who, in the late fourth century—that is, in the early years of the peri–Great Decline and Fall—selected, translated, and compiled the books of Holy Writ that became the Vulgate. It was St. Jerome, in other words, who fashioned the presentation of sacred Scripture that was to become, and still remains, the scriptural canon for Roman Catholism. The thrust of Pius XII's encyclical, however, was to grant permission to the church in general—and to its theologians in particular—to begin to pursue biblical study and scholarship on the basis of original sources, not just on the basis of the Vulgate itself.

At a practical level, what *Divinio* meant was that the largest body in global Christianity, latinized and otherwise, had just given official, sanctioned permission to its faithful to apply twentieth-century tools of textual criticism to their canon and to avail themselves, as well, of all recent and certifiable discoveries, both archaeological and otherwise, including those of previously unknown or previously unavailable manuscripts.[1]

Divinio would be called, by Roman scholars, the Magna Carta of biblical study for the church. By the rest of Christendom, it would be called several other things. Either way, it was seen by all as enabling—and many would say even inviting—a variety of opinions about what was and was not textually accurate and/or authentic. Rome would be the only communion within Christendom to so dramatically grant such overt sanction, but the largest door in the kingdom had been opened, and things probably will never be so sure or certain or absolute again.

At a historical level, *Divinio* was more or less predictable. Every time latinized Christianity has passed through one of its semi-millennial embroilments, the canon has come up for critical review, and reconfiguration and/or redefinition has inevitably followed. The twentieth century in this country had already seen the "invention" of the idea of red-lettered presentation for the words directly attributed as quotes to Jesus, and 1903 had seen the coming of the Scofield Bible with its dispensationalist bent. Midcentury would bring the *Good News Bible* with its joyfully received move of Scripture into the vernacular—or perhaps even in some sections, into the jargon—of the cultural context of its times. Clarence Jordan's the *Cotton Patch Gospel* in the 1970s would move things even farther in that direction, as would dozens of more sedate translations and study Bibles. Indeed, the century would culminate with the much-loved paratranslation, Eugene Peterson's *The Message*.

With so many translations and paratranslations, study Bibles and genre Bibles, annotated Bibles and narrative Bibles, how could anybody—Roman, Protestant, or even just curious—know which and what was the real "real" thing? Yes, there could be no question about the fact that *Divinio Afflante Spiritu* was indeed both right on time and a superb harbinger of things to come.

The Church of the Saviour

But 1943 was not yet done. If it had indeed offered a major indication of things to come for nascent Emergence Christianity in continental Europe, it most certainly may be said to have offered an equally major one for North American Emergence as well. That was the year in which two innovative Christians, Mary and Gordon Cosby, established the Church of the Saviour in Washington, DC. Like the Catholic Worker Houses, Iona, and Taizé, it too was radical. That is, like its fellows, the Church of the Saviour was radical in all the ways that Emergence Christianity was to be increasingly seen as radical by traditional and/or institutionalized Christians. It also chose as well to add a few innovations of its own.

The Cosbys were persuaded that a body of praying, discerning, questing Christians could meet, worship, and meld into community with one another on a sustained, sanctioned, spiritually productive, and holy basis without benefit of an established hierarchy. They contended, as well, that this kind of "church" could be created across any and all denominational lines and could be a servant part of the kingdom without any constrictions of dogmatic or doctrinal loyalties save only those of "Jesus Christ is Son of God" and "Thou shalt love the Lord thy God with all thy heart, all thy mind, all thy strength, and all thy spirit, and thy neighbor as thyself." Such a community could be covenanted, each with the others, while also being flexible enough to hear and respond immediately to the cry of the Spirit and of humanity. To be a member-part of the Church of the Saviour was to accept a call to a radically amorphous and fluid life of faith to the farthest reaches of that word.[2]

To this day, the Church of the Saviour lives, worships, witnesses, and works as this country's earliest example of the gifts that Emergence Christianity can and does bring to the Church Eternal. Incorporated in 1949 with nine people signing the paperwork, Saviour has grown. (It must be noted, and even emphasized, that in good Emergence fashion, growth was never Saviour's aim, much less its measure of success.) But grow it did; and in 1994, it moved to what is called in this country a "scattered communities" format. There is a somewhat more charming Briticism for the same construct called "kirk and chicks." By either name, what's being referenced is a form of horizontal organization in which all members are constituents of both a small church (or chick) and, by extension and active involvement, of the larger and/or mother-henning church. That is, all COTS members are, by covenant, members simultaneously of both a small, tightly bonded, and prayer-bound church of fellow Christians and, by extension, of the larger church or kirk within which the various and scattered communities find their home, their larger fellowship, and often, their respite.

NOTES

1. Textual criticism was already at something rather close to a high boil when *Divinio* was delivered, but that foment was as nothing in comparison to what lay ahead and what *Divinio*, almost presciently, had opened the door for. Heisenburg's articulation of the Principle of Uncertainty in the physics of 1927 would be followed, in formal philosophy, by the coming onto the scene of men like Derrida and Foucault and, in theology, of probing thinkers like Heidegger. By century's end, twentieth-century physics and twentieth-century philosophy together would push secular and religious thought to Deconstruction and beyond. While these things lie outside the bounds of the *Divinio* discussion itself, they should at least be acknowledged here. They certainly will come back into play later, when our attention focuses on the theology of Emergence.

2. One of the most clear-eyed and yet delightfully readable books about the founding and early years of any church or congregation is about the Church of the Saviour, entitled *Call to Commitment: The Story of the Church of the Saviour, Washington, DC*, written by Elizabeth O'Connor. It was published in 1963 by Harper & Row and is still as engaging today as it was almost half a century ago.

7

Taking the Church Out of the Church

Rethinking Sacred Space

Whether in the Belgium of the late 1920s or the Church of the Saviour of later decades, the house church and/or the smaller and/or scattered-communities configuration was to become a hallmark of much of Emergence practice. So too was the idea of a center point: a cohort or place of shared conferring that would keep individual pods from becoming idiosyncratic, isolated, or unavailable for response and mutual discernment. By the 1950s, however, not all of these early Emergence groups (or chicks, if one prefers) were meeting in houses or dedicated spaces, nor were they connected in any way to a kirk. Many of them, especially in Europe and the United Kingdom, were beginning to meet in what the sociologist Ray Oldenburg would call "the third good place." They were, that is, beginning to gather in bars and pubs for study and worship.

Church in a Pub

One of the early examples of this "church in a pub" shift was initiated by the Rev. Tony Reid in the Soho district of London in 1955. The arresting thing about the Soho pub church, beyond the obvious business of its then-unorthodox choice of worship sites, is that Reverend Reid was given permission to pursue his scandalous idea by the rector of St. Anne's, Soho. Father Patrick McLaughlin had heard about the resurgence in Christian faith and practice that had come about in Belgium with the rise of the house church movement. He was no doubt intrigued, but Father Patrick was also a bit of a renegade by disposition. Without any hyperbole being required, it is fair to say, in fact, that Patrick McLaughlin lived and died as one of Britain's most colorful and better-known priests. Some would also say nowadays that he lived and died as an Emergence or, at the very least, a proto-Emergence Christian pioneer.

It was Father McLaughlin who helped to bring theatre back into sacred space by encouraging, and then hosting, productions of such notable playwrights as Christopher Fry. It was McLaughlin who introduced sacred dance into his nave and sought out literary giants like T. S. Eliot to lecture and perform from his pulpit.[1] It was also McLaughlin who, in time, left Anglicanism to become a Roman Catholic priest. Then, not long before his death, he set that aside as well in order to become a lay brother in the Order of St. Benedict. As a career trajectory, nothing could have been more consonant with Emergence sensibilities and convictions than was that of the rector who first sanctioned "church in a pub" as a holy idea and then elected to die as a Benedictine lay brother.

Participatory Liturgy

A year later, in 1956, another quiet innovation took place in America. It appeared at first to be essentially little more than a local adjustment of the status quo, a kind of quaint return to "old" or "European" churchiness. But like the business of taking dance and drama and literature into sacred space, this one, too, saw clearly and early on the swelling desire for aesthetic and participatory liturgy—a desire that, by century's end, would have become a prime hallmark of Emergence Christianity. Peter Hallock, as much as any American church musician—certainly as much as any working within the Episcopal tradition—has made innumerable and unprecedented contributions to liturgical and sacred music over the decades of his long career. None of those contributions may prove to have been as significant, however, as was his decision in 1956 to institute the regular singing of Compline in St. Mark's Cathedral in Seattle.

When Hallock made that move, St. Mark's became the only place outside a monastery or seminary where the office was sung on a regular basis in North America.[2] And they came. The people came. And they still come. In addition, church and cathedral after church and cathedral began to watch the experiment at St. Mark's and then to get the message themselves. In good Emergence fashion, the ancient ways of beauty in worship were on their way to being returned to the ordinary Christian both from within and, in time, also from outside of the institutional church, whatever its particular flavor.[3]

Learning from Monasticism

By the ending months of the 1950s, another expression of communal Emergence would also take visible form in America. Like some kind of homing beam calling them back to the faith's beginnings—to monasticism with its discipline and rich liturgy—its vowed life and Christocentric obedience have, from the beginning, issued a clarion call of the soul to Emergence Christians, becoming for many of them a chosen way of life. Taizé was, and is, built on this very principle as well as upon a sliding scale of involvement and commitment that can go all the way from being a vowed religious to being simply a pilgrim.

Monasteries per se are hierarchal by nature. That is, historically speaking, they exist under the oversight of ecclesial officers like bishops or cardinals or even popes, and they always have. Emergence monasticism, on the other hand, does not desire, much less require, any oversight beyond itself and the discernment in prayer of its own members. The truth, of course, is that if oversight from without is dangerous, so too can the lack thereof be a weakness, if not a danger.

For better or worse, however, Emergence monastic communities functioning under their own authority and/or in coequal communion with other communities constitute one of the major components of Emergence Christianity. Therefore, to distinguish the whole panoply of Emergence monastic practices and adaptations from more familiar and traditional institutional forms, Emergence Christians refer to the sum of their communal bodies as being forms of Neo-monasticism.

Neo-Monasticism

One of the earliest (arguably *the* earliest) of these Neo-monastic communities in North America is the Community of Jesus in Orleans, Massachusetts. Begun in 1959 by two women—an Episcopalian and a Christian Scientist—who were seeking spiritual companionship, healing, and radical obedience to the Spirit, the Community grew from the humble beginning of two families sharing quarters in order to better dedicate themselves to prayer and discernment into what it is today, a community of some three hundred vowed and charismatic brothers, sisters, and lay members.

The route from two women—or Mothers, as they are now called—to a large and almost disproportionately influential body of believers was to prove at times to be a ragged one that involved numerous experiments (most of them later abandoned) in self-organization, external affiliations, and internal authority. In the course of those trial-and-error years, however, the Community birthed, as part of its self and its mission, a touring choir, Gloriæ Dei Cantores; Spirit of America Band; and Paraclete Press, one of this country's more successful religion publishers.

Whether or not a careful study of the Community of Jesus as it moved from a ragtag to a highly liturgical and internally organized body with international affiliations and standing can have any predictive value is more than just a casual question. Now in its sixth decade of existence, the Community quite possibly may furnish religion historians with their earliest case study of what at least the Neo-monastic segment of Emergence Christianity could evolve into, given time. Either way, though, the Community of Jesus was only the first of many vowed groups that would become the Neo-monasticism that is such a visible and effecting part of Emergence Christianity today.[4]

Mega-Church

Before leaving the 1950s, however, it is necessary (for clarity if nothing else) to mention one more thing. Although it did not affect Emergence Christianity per se, the advent in the 1950s of the so-called mega-church construct is at least tangentially related.

Technically speaking, the term *mega-church* refers to the size, not the content, of a Protestant Christian body. It specifically applies to those Protestant churches that have more than two thousand members in regular Sunday attendance. Being purely a mathematical descriptor, it can be correctly applied only to a particular Protestant church on the basis of its congregational size and not of its theological or doctrinal division within the larger rubric of Protestant Christianity itself. All of that having been said, however, it is equally true that the majority of mega-churches in this country are non-denominational in structure and/or evangelical and/or conservative in their theological bent. Those that do retain a connection with a denomination as a rule hold that association very lightly, doing little more than tipping their ecclesial hats toward home base from time to time and usually only upon needful occasions.

Regardless of what form it may take within Protestantism, however, the mega-church is a direct result of the very same cultural pressures and shifts that evoked the Great Emergence itself into being, and it is every bit as much a product of our semi-millennial place in the scheme of things as is Emergence Christianity itself. It is, in other words, an early example of the accommodation and regrouping that always occur within the dominant body of the faith when, in the course of an upheaval, that body begins to lose hegemony or pride of place to new formation within the church.[5]

NOTES

1. We should mention that McLaughlin not only sought to incorporate the aesthetic and the incarnating exercise of the secular as well as the sacred arts into worship, but he also served the artist community pastorally, thus part of his colorful biography. It was he who famously presided over the funeral of Dorothy Sayers, one of twentieth-century Britain's most famous and revered writers of sacred materials as well as some very secular murder mysteries for which she now is better remembered.

2. Taken from a work-in-progress about the Office of Compline by Ken Peterson and relayed to the author by Peterson in an e-letter dated 24 March 2009.

3. The significance here is that one of the growing—perhaps even the fastest-growing—segments of Emergence Christianity is the so-called Hyphenateds, meaning those Christians who want to keep their natal tradition and forms while also wishing to infuse those forms and traditions with Emergence sensibilities. They will be treated in greater depth in coming chapters.

4. To see a splendid photographic essay about the Community today, the reader may want to take advantage of "The Art of Glory" in the October 20, 2010, issue of *Christianity Today* or, better yet, to take advantage of the vibrant presentation of the same material at the magazine's website, www.christianitytoday.com/ct/2010/october/24.34.html. Both the photographs and the accompanying copy are by David Neff.

5. There are well over a thousand Protestant mega-churches in this country and hundreds more abroad. There are also over three thousand Roman Churches in this country that gather in excess of two thousand worshipers each Sunday. Not being Protestant, however, these parishes are more accurately seen simply as "big" rather than "mega." Likewise, there are some Emergence churches in this country that exceed two thousand regular worshipers, Mars Hill in Grand Rapids, Michigan, being the most obvious example.

8

Pentecostal Power

The Holy Spirit in a Dangerous Decade

The 1960s may or may not go down in history as the decade in which America did a sharp, ninety-degree turn from what it had been to some new and at times unrecognizable construct. Regardless of what academic and political history may have to say of the 1960s, however, there is no question about that decade's significance for religion. After all, 1966 was the year that *Time* magazine felt safe and secure enough about the whole thing to announce on its April 8 cover that God was dead.[1] The truth, though, is that the religion shifts, turns, and confusion that *Time* was reflecting had been obvious right from the opening months of that loaded decade.

Van Nuys

It was on Sunday, April 3, 1960, that an Episcopal priest, Father Dennis Bennett, told his Van Nuys parish that he had been baptized in the Spirit. Why the pillars of the building did not fall upon the whole gathered body remains a bit of a mystery, for never, in all of recorded time, had an Anglican or Episcopal priest even felt inclined, much less compelled, to make such a statement from his pulpit on a Sabbath morning to his congregation! The uproar spread quickly out through the church doors and into the surrounding community, making its way in record time to the Van Nuys media and, from there, to the nation's. Azusa Street had come to town. More correctly, Azusa Street had come to dinner and showed every intention of staying around for breakfast as well.

What Bennett did, of course, while it was scandalous in 1960, seems almost ordinary or less than newsworthy to us now, primarily because Azusa Street not only stayed for breakfast but also took up permanent housekeeping among us. But whether scandalous or not, what Bennett was telling his parishioners was that the third party of the Trinity, the Holy Spirit, had flowed upon him in a conscious exchange or engagement and that, as their pastor and chief theologian, he wanted them to understand that he had known the charisms and effects of the so-called second baptism of Pentecost. In sum, he was pentecostal now, though still a priest within the Anglican communion.

The inevitable happened. The pressure of excessive news coverage and the broadcasting of such theological peculiarities forced Bennett to resign from his parish, though not from the priesthood. In fact, he remained a parish priest, though not in Van Nuys, until 1981, when he resigned for the last time in order to give his full energies to the Christian Renewal Association, which, with his wife, Rita, he had established in 1968 and which continues to function today.

One of the greater ironies of religion in the '60s, though, is that when Bennett died in 1991, he died as a Canon of Honor in the church, for during the years from 1960 to 1991, he had spent himself unceasingly in telling what he understood to be "The Story" of our times: the story of the Holy Spirit's coming among us again in visible and corporate form. He gave hundreds of speeches and sermons, more and more of them in increasingly prestigious venues. More to the point, he wrote some half-dozen books that carried his message of a new era in Christian faith to a broad reading public. The most influential of those books, *How to Pray for the Release of the Holy Spirit: What the Baptism or Release of the Holy Spirit Is and How to Pray for It*, is now a classic of the faith whose title says it all.

Charismatic or Pentecostal?

The significance of Dennis Bennett for our purposes here, however, is twofold. First of all, not finding the name of Pentecostal to be a genuinely accurate self-descriptor and not wishing to dissociate himself from Anglicanism either, he lacked a name for what he really was. So, too, did those fellow Christians who were convinced of the truth he was speaking and were beginning to follow him. Among them was a Lutheran pastor, Harald Bredesen, who, in 1962, came up with the idea of "charismatic" as a descriptor. At first blush, that choice seemed a bit unfortunate, however, in that *charismatic* in popular speech denotes one who is unusually attractive in personality and manner and capable of persuading others to his or her point of view. What Bennett and his followers meant, instead, was that they were filled with the Holy Spirit and had received the gifts or charisms of the Spirit, i.e., the speaking in tongues, the gift of healing, the rebirth of baptism, the gift of discernment, etc. Accordingly, the self-generated name was changed simply to "Charismatics" with a capital *C*. What would, within less than thirty years, be a major influence within the larger body of Emergence Christianity had been born.[2]

Second, Charismatics were pentecostals who did not want to be Pentecostals nor to belong to a Pentecostal church or be associated formally with the organization of one. What they wanted instead was to remain within their own natal denominations while at the same time infusing those denominations with the gifts of the Spirit and the ways of Emergence and of Pentecost itself. This approach—that is, to deliberately remain within established church as one who is dedicated to deliberately modifying it or birthing something new out of it—would not only come to denote the differences between Pentecostal and Charismatic Christians, but it would also be an early expression of an attitude that would be unique to Emergence Christianity.

The Hyphenateds

Before the twentieth century's end, one of the larger divisions or component bodies within Emergence Christianity would be the so-called Hyphenateds. They would be persuaded Christians who, like the Charismatics, had little desire to, as they would often say, throw out the baby with the bathwater. Rather, they choose to stay within their established denominations even as they give themselves over to infusing Emergence theology, praxis, and sensibilities into their inherited ways. Historically, such a group has no real precedent, and today they constitute one of the open-ended questions we shall treat later about where Emergence is going and what, when fully grown, it may turn out to be.[3]

Vatican II

Even as Hyphenateds were beginning to emerge and as Charismatics were finding their own new place in the sun, the oldest body within latinized Christianity was once again preparing to come to grips with the growing pressures of changing cultures and shifting times. Four months after he was elected to the papacy in 1958,

Pope John XXIII announced to the church that his intention was to convoke a second Vatican Council; and on October 11, 1962, he did just that. Vatican II would remain actively in place until it was officially closed on December 8, 1965, by John XXIII's successor, Pope Paul VI.

Whole books have been written about Vatican II, and no doubt many more will be. Despite all of those books, however, there will probably never be any consensus about exactly what the Council did or did not do, much less about what it did or did not permit and/or sanction. In all of the confusion, however, one thing is very clear: Vatican II changed Roman Catholicism completely and, by extension of attitude and influence, latinized Christianity as well.

Among some of the other relevant and very clear things about Vatican II is the fact that, without question, the Council was convoked as a way of addressing the shifts and upheavals of a new "re-formation," to borrow Walter Rauschenbusch's term for it. In his opening address to the Second Session of Vatican II in 1963, Pope Paul VI listed his agenda as being geared toward four things in particular, all of them pertinent here: the Council was to define the nature of the church; it was to act as a means and mechanism for renewing the church; it was to seek all possible means of achieving unity among all the branches of Christianity, including even going so far as to apologize for Rome's part in having created division in the first place[4]; and above all else, it was to initiate genuine and efficacious dialogue with the contemporary world as it really was, not as churchmen might wish it to be.

In effect and in response to the times, Vatican II was to be an attempt to return much of the authority in the church to the people who were the church, and in doing so, it was being asked as well to redefine authority itself, especially the authority and role of the past writings, positions, theologians, Fathers, and Councils of the historic church. As questions, issues, and subjects of deliberation, these points of contention would prove, over the coming decades, hardly to be unique to Roman Christianity. Rather, they would be ubiquitous in all parts of both the general and the Emergence conversation. In the end, they would become the core of a central, overarching question: "Where now is our authority?" or more gently put, "How now shall we live?"

Globalization

Additionally but far less intentionally, the Council, by its very composition, evidenced another shift of peri-Emergence times, namely that toward globalization. That is, a substantial number of the bishops gathered at Vatican II were no longer southern Europeans. Instead, many were from northern Europe. Perhaps more significantly, over a hundred of them were from Africa, Latin America, and Asia. By their very numbers, they reflected not only the changing face of Roman Catholicism but also the changing face of the latinized Christian world and of the larger world in general. As a result, the need to consider in councilor form the role of Christianity in a multifaith world and of the Roman Church in a multiform Christianity was not so much a need as it was an imperative. Those very questions would, of course, soon come to besiege almost every single group within Christendom, just as they continue to the present day as areas of ongoing discussion among Emergence thinkers and theologs.

Nor can we leave Vatican II without contextualizing it in yet one other way, one that even the presiding popes themselves probably did not fully grasp at the time: by its very existence, its choice of emphases, and particularity its shift to a more globalized constituency, Vatican II tentatively cracked open the theological and ecclesial doors of the Roman Church for the entrance and eventual mainstreaming of a line of social and political argument that we would eventually come to know as *liberation theology*. Liberation theology would have its greatest overt impact in Latin America.

As a code of values and a covenant of theologically argued action, however, and like the work of Dorothy Day and Peter Maurin, it would become, within a matter of just a few years, a powerful and active component within a massive sociopolitical upheaval that was both religious in its origins and in its consequences.

In 1968 and less than three full years after Paul VI closed Vatican II, Martin Luther King Jr. was assassinated in a martyrdom that shook the Americas to the very core of their beliefs, self-image, values, and structures. The power of nonviolent protest and the drive toward equal freedom for all people that had started in India with Ghandi now became almost a latinized faith or religion in and of themselves. The concept of civil rights was no longer a dandified theory or a line of intellectualized morality. It was here.

Bought in King's blood, it was here.

And a year later, in 1969, James Cone would define for the whole world just what it was that was. He would publish *Black Theology and Black Power*, arguably one of the twentieth century's most seminal books and certainly the one that, as its title suggests, juxtaposed theological argument and political action into one dramatic but effectual whole.

Liberation Theology

Only six years after the closure of Vatican II and three years after King's slaughter, a Peruvian priest, Father Gustavo Gutierrez, speaking out of the possibilities of Vatican II, the anguish of the times in general, and his own culture in particular, also published a book. It was entitled *A Theology of Liberation*. The thing that had been hinted at within Vatican II now had a name. Liberation theology had been, if not exactly born, then most certainly christened. It would be expanded by the works of other brilliant theologians like Leonardo Boff and Jon Sobrino, but as with civil rights, so with liberation theology. It would most fully come to be only after 1980. In March of that year, Bishop Oscar Romero would be slaughtered in El Salvador for his promulgation of liberation theology. Blood once more would be the price paid for universal presence.

Women's rights and feminist theology, though less violent in their evolution, function among us today as expressions of this same push toward an egalitarian stance in both church and state as well as in culture and society. They are, however—or so most would argue—less completely realized parts of liberation thought and implementation. Beyond any question, however, one last event within 1969 still remains without resolution. In June 1969, at Stonewall Inn in Greenwich Village, a group of homosexuals physically resisted police harassment, and the series of riots that followed ruptured history. That is, they forced into public discussion the last barrier to full equality among human beings—regardless of one's views of homosexual sex.

The rightness of the gay, lesbian, bisexual, and transgendered life, much less the rights of those who so live, was to dominate cultural conversations for decades. It certainly was to thrust latinized Christian theology and ecclesiology into a divisive turmoil that has not yet reached resolution. In many ways, though, the implications of this battle are more ferociously telling than were the implications and consequences of all the others. That is, the injunction against homosexuality in all its forms is the last of the biblically based injunctions still standing in the latinized world. Should it come to be resolved, the doctrine of Protestant inerrancy will have no other battlefield on which to defend itself. The die will have been cast and the Rubicon crossed.

Any discussion of social justice cannot end here, however. There is one more very telling thing that must be mentioned: social justice, within less than three decades after Stonewall, would become a kind of acid test for separating established Christianity groups from Emergence Christianity ones.

Unquestionably, both groups fought hard for the social and legal equality we now enjoy in North America. Roman Catholicism, without a doubt, was in the vanguard of those changes from the very onset of the twentieth century. Equally true is the fact that Protestant activists and theologians were just as vigorously behind the effecting of those changes as were their Roman coreligionists. Almost all older Emergence Christians (of whom there are increasing numbers, as a matter of fact) were every bit as adamant, if not more so. The difference for the Emergence Christians, however, was that most of them did not yet name themselves as Emergence Christians and simply took up their stances as part of the push by the established church. But the ground shifted.

Once the long-sought changes had begun to become, if not goals, then the rules of the game, two things happened. First, many (and, one could argue, even most) established and/or traditional church congregations and bodies, while they still believed earnestly in social justice and continued to fight for it with their words, money, and time, were less ready to welcome the results into their space, their worship, and their lives. The former "other-thans" who had been recently enfranchised were to be honored and respected, just not comfortably incorporated into everyday private or spiritual or communal life. Social justice was something one did for other human beings; it was not something one did for one's self.

For proto-Emergence Christians, though, the story was different. The battles for equality of all were—and are—battles for the fullness of life and worship that comes to all people when we are all together in every part of our common lives. That distinction was to become one of the more obvious and principal differences between established church and Emergence.

The second divisive consequence of the push for social justice was less subtle. While Christian activists of all persuasions had argued theologically for the rightness of their cause, evangelical Christians of all denominational persuasions began to argue biblically against the correctness of some of those changes. Liberal vs. conservative as fighting words came into play. But what had also come among us was the first major intrafamilial tussle within American evangelicalism. The tussle would eventually become a civil war, and it would affect Emergence almost as much as evangelicalism itself.

NOTES

1. While decades later most of us tend to be flip—as I have been here—about that famous cover and *Time*'s sangfroid in publishing it, the truth is that its appearance is a major mile-marker in American religion, just as it was a significant indicator of the changes that were already afoot and that would soon be spoken of as Emergence Christianity. One of the keenest commentaries and richest explications currently available on all of this is Karen Armstrong's *The Case for God* (Alfred A. Knopf, 2009).

2. There is a humorous story (whether mythical or true, I don't know) that Pastor Bredesen was frightened into his invention of capital C Charismatics as a name because folk had begun to refer to him as a "neo-Pentecostal," a titling that he apparently found to be even more abhorrent than the misnomer of just plain Pentecostal.

What might—or might not, actually—have amused Pastor Bredesen is the fact that all his efforts may yet prove to have been in vain. Commencing in about 2007 or 2008, respected demographers and students of religion like the Pew Foundation began, for statistical reasons, to lump Pentecostals and Charismatics together in their reports under the larger rubric of "Renewalists." That larger term is now being used increasingly because of its sheer convenience, even if that use does blur a very real distinction.

3. *Hyphenateds* as a name had its origin in the 1990s when such groups defined themselves as presby-mergents or bapto-mergents or luther-mergents or catho-mergents or angli-mergents, etc. By the turn of this century, the hyphens had all disappeared, but the name has held on. Thus, we now have presbymergents, baptomergents, luthermergents, cathomergents, anglimergents, etc.

4. Another sign of the times that was ironic and timely as well as bittersweet was a joint statement, just as Vatican II was closing, by Paul VI and the Orthodox Patriarch Athenagoras, in which the two expressed their mutual regret for many of the actions that had led up to, and finally tripped, the Great Schism of the eleventh century.

9

Spiritual but Not Religious

Belonging, Behaving, and Believing in a New Kind of Community

The 1960s were a decade of violence, certainly, and it was a violence that would form the eventual shape of the Great Emergence and of Emergence Christianity in particular. But to leave the 1960s there as if they had contributed only turmoil and division would be to ignore another of their prime characteristics. The 1960s were colorful—wondrously, self-indulgently colorful. They were also daring, or perhaps one might better say that much of their color came from their inherent predisposition toward daring.

Theologically, if that is the correct term here, those years were a veritable hotbed of new ideas and even of some old ones, revisited and revamped. The 1960s brought into popular conversation the concept of the Age of Aquarius, the mantra of "I'm spiritual but not religious," and the suggestive fascination of a refurbished and modernized Wicca. While each of them is a distinctly definable construct, they all held in common, and continue to hold in common, the seductive appeal of being just beyond the limits of the previously acceptable.

The Dawning of the Age of Aquarius

The Age of Aquarius was, first and foremost, the wailing cry of an age and culture that understood in some dumb or mute kind of way that times were changing in a disorienting and cataclysmic fashion. There was, in fact, a barrage of change that wanted explanation and purpose if one were to survive the whole thing. And whatever else it was or may be, the talk of the Age of Aquarius, which continues to this day, is a reaching back to prescientific, pre-Enlightenment wisdom and astrological lore as a way to understand and, by understanding, to manipulate to some greater or lesser extent the courses of life.

The Age of Aquarius exploration would come to be either discounted or else outright condemned as a rebirth of Gnosticism by most Christian bodies. For their trouble, those same Christian groups would cease to be of any importance to thousands of people who left them in order to seek comfort and direction where at least the problem was being openly recognized and, for better or worse, addressed and engaged. Having left "church," however, many of those thousands would also come eventually to find that Aquarian thinking was not exactly to their liking either. Or, simply finding it unsatisfying, they would come to seek instead a conversation that was open to their concerns but still rooted in a familiar and theistic faith.

Church as institution and tradition had failed them by failing both to engage and to evolve, but . . .

Ah, but . . . but there was a new feeling abroad, a new sensibility, a new conversation that spoke in Jesus terms, yet not with the restrictions of dogma and enculturated doctrine. There were these little pockets of people who believed—and believed radically—yet were not afraid to question because they were responsible to no institutional policies regarding conversation.

Even if one found no home within Aquarian thought or Aquarian groups, one could still feel the restiveness and discontent that Aquarius addressed. Certainly, one could still feel—and resent, as well—the inadequacy of the institution that was supposed to salve restiveness and ease discontent. Yet by and large, the Institution and/or the institutions that were its physical presence could not bend enough to admit of the restiveness, and what cannot be acknowledged cannot be engaged. So why not look elsewhere? Why not look at meaning and purpose and explanation and faith wherever they have existed and do exist? Why not push on beyond religion and get to the Holy? Why not become spiritual instead of religious? Why not indeed?

The business of being spiritual instead of religious proved to be more satisfying in general than did that of being an Aquarian in particular, at least for the greater percentage of people. As a result, somewhere between a quarter and a third of Americans today will still describe themselves to pollsters and demographers as "spiritual but not religious." In defining "not religious," though, what is often meant might more clearly be defined as "unchurched." That is, what is often meant is that there is no official membership or even casual attendance in an established place of worship. Instead, there is, for many such people, a simple gathering with friends for talking about the spiritual life as one knows it in Jesus and God. There is singing and praise using Christian words in small groups or even in larger gatherings or even more or less consistently. There is participation in green causes and social justice and generous events of service to one's fellows in need. There is a good deal of reading and communal pondering of Scripture and a lot of prayer. There is Emergence Christianity, but it is spiritual Christ-knowing, not religion.[1]

John Wimber

As surely, though, as the 1960s did not suffer from any lack of colorful ideas and movements, so too did it not suffer from any lack of colorful public figures. And in the shaping of Emergence Christianity during that decade, there was not—and probably never could be—any more colorful an innovator than was John Wimber. Indeed, were it possible to play one of those parlor games of "Whom do you most wish you had gotten to meet, but didn't?" John Wimber would be the first choice for many younger historians of contemporary religion. He was a walking contradiction, a walking amazement, and before he was done, a walking holy man.

John was, in the early 1960s, a cavalier and well-positioned musician, a keyboard player for the Paramours and, many say, the impetus or enabler behind the formation of the Righteous Brothers. He knew the world, and he knew how to work it. But then, in 1963, in Yorba Linda, California, he and his wife converted to Christianity. They converted, in fact, to Quakerism, and Wimber's understanding of "the world" changed almost instantaneously from a secular concept to a kingdom one.

Over the next few years, the Wimbers would gradually move from being Quakers to being part of a worship and study group that was meeting in their house and worshiping under his leadership. By 1974, he would be teaching at Fuller Seminary in Pasadena, serving as founding director of the Department of Church Growth there until 1978, when he began what was, in time, to become the Anaheim Vineyard Church. Everything about Wimber was Emergence, from the early and formative influence of Quakerism to the almost accidental establishment of a house church in his home, to his formal association with Fuller, and then to the Vineyard movement that, to all intents and purposes, he founded.

One of the rather engaging side trips one can take in studying Emergence's formative years is to take a look at the bodies and configurations that came about in those late midcentury decades when nonhierarchal organization was not yet quite conceivable despite the fact that denominational hierarchy was no longer acceptable. The Vineyard, which is now a vast and international gathering of Christians, still names itself as an "association," thus denying any suggestion of its being a denomination in the old sense while, at the same time, asserting that it nonetheless has shape and form. Other groups, like Calvary Chapels or Willow Creek, for instance, have followed the same pattern in their evolution.

Wimber, however, was far too seminal a thinker for his influence to remain confined in one association or restricted to one mode of thinking. Deeply charismatic, he saw a large part of his call as having to do with the reviving and/or redirecting of evangelicalism. Specifically, he sought to guide evangelicals into practices, attitudes, and postures that were more robust and spiritual than were the doctrinal squabbles and rampant politicization that had begun to characterize evangelicalism as a communion or mind-set within contemporary latinized Christianity. He coined the phrase "empowered evangelicals," in fact, in order to try to effect and then name the merger of the two postures of evangelicalism and Pentecostalism.

Ecclesially, one of Wimber's great contributions to Emergence was his positioning of center-set/bound-set thinking as central to Christian practice. That is, he insisted that Christian bodies must take the position that everyone who wants to come thereby belongs just because of the wanting and without regard to how he or she may behave or claim to believe. Such a position was a complete reversal of the historic and institutionalized posture that one must believe and attest to certain things and agree to behave in a certain way before being allowed to join or belong. In effect, the old, sociological formula of Believe/Behave/Belong was reversed to become Belong/Behave/Believe.

Wimber also affected Emergence's worship praxis. Principally, he taught the importance of discernment within a gathered group.

He insisted on the extended teaching lesson as opposed to the long-established pattern of the twenty-minute homily. He encouraged conversation and critique following a congregational lesson, and above all else, he believed in the power of music to open the soul and rejoice the Spirit of God. In other words, anyone who pursues the course of an emerging Emergence Christianity will trip, time and time again, over the name and/or hand of John Wimber.

And there were certainly other contemporaries of Wimber who were beginning to take scholarly note of what was happening and to name it as well. By the mid-to-late 1960s, academic observers like Wolfhart Pannenberg in Germany and Wade Clark Roof in the United States were beginning to give historical and predictive analysis to what was happening and why, as well as to where it all might be assumed to be going, at least in the near future.[2] Even more interesting and telling, however, may once again have been an acknowledgment by Rome that new things were afoot.

On June 5, 1968, under full imprimatur and with an advisory board of ten monsignors and sitting bishops, William J. Kalt and Ronald J. Wilkins, with the special assistance of Dr. Raymond Schmandt, published a book entitled *The Emerging Church, Part One*.[3] If there were no other reason at all, the book would still be of significance simply because it appears to have been the first published work of consequence to employ the term *Emerging Church* in its title.

The greater significance for our purposes here, however, rests in the fact that Kalt and Wilkins's work is the sixth volume in a series entitled *To Live in Christ*, a series that was created for the express purpose of Catholic adult education and formation. True to the tenor of Vatican II and no doubt empowered by it, Kalt and Wilkins's volume is also sympathetically and cordially inclined toward the Emerging Church it presents. Rome had indeed been here before, but she had learned from past experience, and it was serving her well.[4]

NOTES

1. Probably no other area of recent religious history in this country has received more scholarly study than has the "spiritual but not religious" phenomenon. Some of our most astute sociologists as well as gifted theologians have addressed it, and any attempt to give a full bibliography here would be beyond the scope of this book. Instead, the interested reader may wish to look at *Spiritual, but not Religious: Understanding Unchurched America* (Oxford University Press, 2001) by Robert C. Fuller. Fuller's work is not only generous in its content, it is also very generous in its review of extant literature on the subject and in its bibliography.

One other thing must also be noted here. That is, unlike Aquarian thinking and spiritual-but-not-religious thinking, the Wicca of the '60s has managed to retain a goodly number of its converts. It certainly continues today as a marginal, but earnest and active, presence in both American and Continental religion. Its greatest effect upon institutional church, and quite possibly upon Emergence Christianity as well, is not only its draining away of older and disaffected former practicing Christians and cultural Christians but also its enormous appeal to twenty-first-century teens and young adults. Part of that appeal is that Wicca speaks directly to a concern that is central to, and ubiquitous within, the Great Emergence. That is, it speaks to a deep and politicized as well as theologized concern for the Earth, which is Greenness for non-Wiccans and Mother, Goddess, and Divinity without equal for Wiccans.

2. For an extended discussion of this material, see my *The Great Emergence: How Christianity Is Changing and Why* (Baker, 2008), 125ff.

3. Henry Regnery, 1968.

4. It is worthy of note as well that, so far as I can ascertain, Kalt and Wilkins were the first to lay out our semi-millennial cycling patterns as being of importance in lay education (52ff). They, however, name the five-hundred-year periods rather than the upheavals themselves. Thus, the time from 500 to 1000 CE is titled Reconstruction Christianity; 1000 to 1500 CE is Medieval Christianity; and amusingly enough, at least to Protestants, the unfortunate years from 1500 to the present are divided into Renaissance Christianity (1500 to ca. 1700 CE) and Modern Christianity (1700 to 1960 CE).

10

What the Hyphen Means

Claiming the New While Honoring the Old

As was true in the late nineteenth century with Vatican I and the Niagara meetings that followed hard on its heels, so it was in the twentieth century. In 1970, only five years after Vatican II and two after Kalt and Wilkins, Word Publishing, an influential Protestant house, released *The Emerging Church* by Ralph Larson and Bruce Osbourne. Now, incontestably, even the most chary observer could say that the two largest bodies within latinized Christianity—Roman Catholicism and Protestantism—had both begun to acknowledge by name this new thing that was.

Also in 1970 (and perhaps even more significantly over the long haul of history), the first self-consciously "hyphenated" church was born. St. Gregory of Nyssa, established in a barrio of San Francisco by two Episcopal priests—Father Donald Schell and Father Rick Fabian—was, from its inception, quintessentially Emergence. As such, it would function for over thirty years without becoming officially connected to the Episcopal Church in any way, although it now enjoys a more customary relationship with the larger church even as it remains very much a thing unto itself.

Deeply involved in social justice and radical, egalitarian charity, St. Gregory's is incarnational in the accoutrements of its worship and its use of music. It is liturgical in a way more resonant of the first few centuries of the church than of more recent times, and it borrows heavily from the traditions and habits of Orthodox and Coptic Christianity. It is, in every way, the quintessential example of a Hyphenated—or to be more specific, of an anglimergent—community.

Because the Hyphenateds and the Neo-monastics are the two groups or divisions within Emergence that present currently as the fastest-growing segments thereof, and because we have in St. Gregory's and in the Community of Jesus two of the oldest Emergence bodies in the United States, the two of them are increasingly objects of interest and study for those who are trying to discern where Emergence may be going and what it may reasonably be expected to look and function like in its maturity.

Music Festivals

But Emergence Christianity in the '70s was still a fairly innocent and newborn thing. And like all young things, there was a certain joie de vivre that accrued, in addition to the kind of deadly seriousness we often assign to it. The need to celebrate, to sing, to cry out and be glad was as much a part of Emergence's birthing years as were those other, more ponderous issues. That was (and is) entirely as it should be, for it has always been music that has carried religion, that has transmitted the faith, and that has excited the soul and spirit beyond the sometimes-burdensome particularities of dogma and doctrine. So it was that, in 1974, Greenbelt—or, more properly, the Greenbelt Festival—was born.[1]

Other festivals would follow. The Jesus People would start the Cornerstone Festival in the United States in 1984. SLOT would be created in Poland. There would be the Black Stump Festival in Australia, and in an attempt to create a United States Greenbelt of sorts, the Wild Goose Festival would be inaugurated in 2011 in the States. But regardless of how many look-alikes and other-thans there may be, Greenbelt remains as the granddaddy of them all.[2]

In excess of twenty thousand Emergence Christians from all over the latinized world gather every year at the grounds of Cheltenham Racetrack outside of London to spend four days camping out in tents and RVs in order to sing together and be sung to, worship together, praise together, learn together, listen together, and in general become as one together.

In the same way that camp meetings were an energetic and galvanizing part of Christian life in much of this country during the eighteenth and nineteenth centuries, so too with Greenbelt. It was the first global statement by Emergences of all persuasions that "We are!" It fused—and continues to this day to fuse—disparate Christians drawn from disparate parts of old Christendom into a coherent whole, if not for a lifetime, then at least for a few days. It is as near "central" in a geographic or physical sense as Emergence is likely ever to get. It certainly was the one single thing that granted the greatest cohesion to Emergence in the 1970s and 1980s.

"The Church of the Catacombs"

But the 1970s and the place and status of Emergence Christianity as that decade ended are probably best summarized in the words of that far from universally appreciated bishop Jack Spong, senior churchman, astute analyst of all things in religion, and curmudgeon who has never been known to pull any punches when speaking about Christianity. In the January 3–10, 1979, issue of the venerable *Christian Century* magazine, Spong published an article entitled "The Emerging Church: A New Form for a New Era." It was his subtitle, however, that was the ringer. That subtitle read "The Institutional

Shape of the Church in History Is Always Determined by the Attitude of the World Toward That Which the Church Professes."

In his closing paragraph, Spong wrote:

> We are living at the time of the birth of a new Christian consensus which someday will be studied alongside the church of the catacombs, or the age of the great cathedrals, or the time of the church as the center of religious life. That emerging church, I believe, will combine elements. . . . A new shape for the church will be born in human history. It will be as different from the traditional church of our experience as the great cathedrals were from the church in the catacombs.

Bishop Spong concluded that paragraph and his essay with the words:

> And Christians will recognize that continuity when they call the new shape and form of the body of Christ living in the 21st century a church.

Doubtless, there is little more that could be added either then or now.

NOTES

1. Greenbelt has often been referred to as "the Christian's Woodstock," and for apt reason. Woodstock, when it happened in August of 1969, was presented as "An Aquarian Exposition" and was deliberately structured to function as a full-sensory, spiritual experience. Over and over again, any student of religion comes upon the hard fact that it is music that most effectually carries new concepts of religion into the believer. Even Martin Luther of Reformation sobriety and somberness has been called "the first reforming rapper." To prove that point, *Christian Century* quotes Luther as having said he used rhyme, meter, and melody to teach the new creeds and theology and "to give the young . . . something to wean them away from love ballads and carnal songs and teach them something of value in their place" (May 2011, 17). *Sic simper est.*

2. The recognition of the importance of this kind of religious celebration has grown so substantially over the last quarter century that there is now an Association of Christian Festivals. A quick perusal of the association's membership roster is a fairly dramatic introduction to the magnitude of the phenomenon.

11

Innocence Lost

A Movement Untethered

The 1980s were a time almost of hesitation, or perhaps constituted by what a poet once called "the brink of an exquisite indecision." For institutional church in the United States, it was the time of the full flowering of the Religious Right that had begun in the late '70s and would enter the '90s as a divisive force within not only American politics but also within American Christianity. Evangelicals, regardless of their denominational affiliations, would be pulled apart and severed into two incompatible bodies of belief about what Scripture says and, after that, into other differences about where and how what it says should be applied. Christendom—that craggy old institution that had held firm since Constantine and the Milvian Bridge—would begin to show the first telltale signs of its approaching decrepitude and, before century's end, of its demise. But for Emergence Christians, there was a kind of young sweetness to the '80s, although those years would lay the groundwork for what in the '90s would be the heartbreak of its first shameful disaster.

Johann Baptist Metz

Things began well. In 1981, Johann Baptist Metz, a prominent German theologian, student of Karl Rahner, and among other things, a major influence in the shaping of liberation theology, produced a work entitled, in its English edition, *The Emergent Church: The Future of Christianity in a Postbourgeois World*. In it, Metz predicts—or perhaps, better said, he recognizes and articulates the fact—that this new construct in latinized Christianity will come up from the grass roots and not from the so-called established middle class of Reformation origins. While Metz's work may not have shaken the world or been so broadly read as, for instance, Spong's work, it nonetheless stands as a landmark. A major theologian had addressed Emergence in a scholarly treatment not only of its religious but also of its sociological makeup and implications. Emergence—because it is, as Metz observed, postbourgeois—probably could not have cared less, but the larger world had to. A kind of credential or writ of credibility had been granted, and that could not be ignored.

Robert Webber

At about the same time and in the United States, Robert Webber, a much-loved and respected academic theologian, was beginning to speak popularly about what he perceived as "the call to the ancient-future." To this day and several years after his death, the term *ancient-future* still evokes memories of Webber and of his acumen in being the first to give both diagnosis and voice to what is now a principal characteristic of Emergence Christianity in all its forms. We are, he said, filled with a yearning to go back, to rediscover for ourselves what it was that was worth dying for, what it meant to worship in small covens of outcasts and the rejected, and what it was like to have intimate contact with the thoughts and meditations of the fathers and mothers of the faith. We are, in other words, he said, rapidly hastening toward the third century. We are in pursuit of the ancient-future.

It was a brilliant summation of what was happening, and Webber was to expand upon it in 1985, when he wrote what is now a classic of Emergence history, *Evangelicals on the Canterbury Trail*. In it, he argues that it is Anglicanism—thus the "Canterbury" in the title—that holds, with the greatest impunity, the treasures of the church's past. Rome is still too hierarchal. Protestantism is, in a sense, the thing from which Emergent Christians are fleeing. Orthodoxy is still too outré or unfamiliar in Europe and the Americas. Only Anglicanism can claim both a fairly neutral (for Emergences, anyway) history and a more or less direct or unbroken line with early forms and expressions of latinized Christianity. Basically, Webber was so correct in his analysis that more than one wit has observed that his only mistake was in using the word *evangelicals*. It was and is Emergences, many of whom are indeed natal evangelicals, who travel the Canterbury Trail.[1]

Webber, who died in 2008, had also put his finger on the other issue that would increase in visibility and significance. In conflating Emergences and evangelicals—or perhaps in not seeing the Emergences as other than, or different from, the then-more-visible evangelicals—he had not only reflected a prominent confusion in his time, but he had also managed to call attention, albeit unintentionally, to the painful distinction that was simmering its way toward a full-blown boil. Within twenty years of *Canterbury Trail*'s release, evangelicalism and/or evangelicals would be probing the distinctions between themselves and Emergence, the former increasingly seeing the latter as a threat or as ecclesial poachers, even. Friendships would rupture and, by 2010, battle lines would begin to be drawn. That, however, was not the sudden sadness that would commence in the '80s and come to an end in the '90s. The sudden sadness was a thing called the Nine O'Clock Service and the painful realization that Emergence, too, could stumble and fall down.[2]

Signs and Wonders

In 1985, John Wimber led a Signs and Wonders conference in Sheffield, England. It was quintessential Wimber in its passion for Christ and its pentecostal, nondenominational, all-accepting, music-laden approach. It was also "successful," if that term may be appropriately applied to spiritual experience. However that may be, though, it is still true that many of the people who participated in the Sheffield Signs and Wonders conference did not want to go back to their normal lives as if nothing had happened. They wished, instead, to continue as a worshiping body and spiritual family bound to one another by sustained prayer and deliberate praxis. Accordingly, in 1986, a group of them began to worship together as a discrete body or unit of believers. Just as significant, ultimately, was the fact that they were granted space for their worship within the walls of St. Thomas's Church in Sheffield.

Nine O'Clock Service

Under the leadership of one of their own members, a lay Christian named Chris Brain, the group's original intention was to create an alternative worship format that would more or less follow the Vineyard pattern and emphases. Accordingly, Brain and some of his friends began to devise a worship service that, when completed, met with the approval of St. Thomas's rector and of its parish council as well as, ultimately, that of the bishop of Sheffield himself. With continued meeting facilities more or less guaranteed by St. Thomas, the group began to grow. In the due course of things, they came to name themselves the Nine O'Clock Service as a way to distinguish their form of alternative worship from that of the Sabbath services attended by the rest of St. Thomas's faithful. By 1988, there was a problem, however.

Brain had proved to be a mesmerizing and very charismatic leader, in the most secular sense of that lowercase *c* word. NOS now had six hundred congregants and, as a result, had completely outgrown St. Thomas's facilities. The group moved, and things began to fall apart.

In their new quarters at Pond's Forge, outside of Sheffield, Brain and the congregation were at a remove from direct pastoral or episcopal oversight. Although Brain himself had agreed to study for orders as an ordained Anglican priest, he now became more and more absorbed with the "alternative" part of alternative worship, eventually creating what came to be called the *Planetary Mass*. By 1993, the *Mass* would attract the attention, and ultimately the participation, of Matthew Fox, a former American Dominican and Roman Catholic priest. Prior to his coming to Sheffield, Fox had already fallen crosswise of Rome for his heterodox ideas and had been defrocked for his trouble by a man known at that time as Joseph Cardinal Ratzinger.[3]

Over the ensuing months, the *Planetary Mass* experience as it was practiced in Sheffield became more and more involved in raves and other experimental worship forms, even as it became farther and farther separated from orthodox Christian belief. Then, within a short time, it began to veer more and more into a variant that might best be described as sexual and/or magical mysticism. Despite this devolvement into darkness and disorder, NOS still continued to operate under the aegis of the Church of England, though by now it was totally without any kind of church oversight, clerical contact, or physical proximity.

Congregational numbers began to drop, coming eventually to be no more than half of what they had once been. Yet, despite the mounting and increasingly obvious aberrations and difficulties, some three hundred folk remained. Those who stayed formed themselves into—or, as many would later claim, were forced by Brain into—a cultlike, highly secretive body of the psychologically manipulated. Things escalated into more and more abusive behavior and finally burst apart into scandal for all, shame and disenchantment for many, and psychiatric hospitalization for Brain.

Emergence Christianity had had its first lesson in the devastating consequences of straying too far from Mother Church. Likewise, Mother Church, in the shape of the Church of England, had learned her own bitter lesson about just how far she could extend her license without retaining supervision over its use. That lesson, so well and painfully learned, would inform and shape Church of England policy toward Emergence for the next two decades and, in all probability, for all the decades after that, as we shall soon see.

NOTES

1. As it turns out, the connection that Webber saw between Anglicanism and Emergence has proved to be not only very operative but also mutually beneficial in almost precisely the ways that Webber envisioned. Anglican liturgy is based upon the ancient liturgies of the faith as they have come to be formalized in *The Book of Common Prayer*, regardless of which country or language any given edition of the BCP may be in use. With few exceptions, the contents vary from one language edition to another only in language. Additionally, and again with only one or two exceptions, no rending of the BCP bears a copyright, making it available, thereby, for any who wish to follow it or amend it or even modify it to accommodate particular purposes. As a result, one quite frequently finds snatches—sometimes even great swaths—of Anglican form folded into Emergence Christian worship.

In May of 2010, Brian McLaren furnished the foreword to a paper entitled "Seize the Episcopal Moment: An Emergent Manifesto of Hope for the Episcopal Church." Principally written by Karen Ward, then abbess of the Church of the Apostles in Seattle, with Fr. Donald Schell, cofounding priest of St. Gregory of Nyssa in San Francisco, the paper is still widely circulated and also easily available on the web. It is, however, McLaren's foreword that is the most revelatory of the nature of the present interchange between Emergence and Anglican Christianity.

2. The full story of the Nine O'Clock Service exceeds the limits of an overview like this one. It is, nonetheless, a story worth telling. Those who are interested will find a complete history of it in *Rise and Fall of the Nine O'Clock Service* by Roland Howard (Mowbray, 1996).

3. As for Matthew Fox himself, he returned to the United States, where his development of Creation Spirituality and his instituting of rave and Cosmic Masses garnered him not only an almost unprecedented amount of general media coverage but also a substantial and continuing body of followers and supporters. He still continues his work with sustained energy, just as he has continued his fight with Rome and, in particular, with his old nemesis Ratzinger, now Pope Benedict XVI. In 2005, shortly after Ratzinger's election to the papacy, Fox again garnered huge media coverage by drawing up his own set of Ninety-Five Theses calling for a new Reformation and then nailing them to the door of the church in Wittenberg, Germany, just as Luther had done almost five hundred years earlier with his own declaration of reformation.

12

Religion Rebounds

Gathering Steam and Getting a Name

The '90s were to evolve into a time of cultural soul-searching and, before they were over and done, into a time of political despair for Americans in general. But in their beginning, in those first four or five years of the decade, the '90s were to be almost obsessively involved with questions and ideas about religion on a felt and personal level.

Religion books rose to the top of bestsellers lists, and for most of those early years, book wholesalers reported triple-digit growth annually in the amount of religion product moving through them to the nation's bookstores and libraries. The stream of culture-wide conversation was not organized or vetted or sanctified or certified by much of anybody, but it was experiential religion in as many shapes and forms as even the most inventive soul could ever hope to imagine. As a culture, we all got embraced by angels and touched by the light wherever we went. We loved everything Celtic and green, lit candles even in the most unlikely places, and believed earnestly in the efficacy or benefits of holy icons as refrigerator magnets.

It was a strange time—a singular time, in fact—and if it lacked cohesion or sometimes even credible content, it did not lack for generative promise. Whatever else was happening in all that chaos, one thing is retrospectively clear: Emergence Christianity was becoming. It was wrenching itself loose from the religious mélange in which it had been resting, and in its wrenching, it was becoming self-aware. Writing some fifteen years later in 2009, Andrew Jones, one of Emergence's better-known and more acerbic chroniclers, put it another way. Jones wrote that 1994 was the year that "the trickle became a stream" for Americans.[1]

By the closing years of the century, Jones's stream had become a river of sorts. And one of the more obvious things that that river was doing was transporting an alarming number of eighteen-to-thirty-five-year-old Americans straight out of established churches and into these strange new "whatevers" that were happening in strange old places like yoga studios and public parks and tawdry music halls.

The Leadership Network

The Leadership Network was, and is, a highly respected national organization within North American evangelicalism. Its primary purpose, as its name suggests, is to serve the Christian tradition by dedicating itself to the development and continuing formation and education of evangelical leaders. As the larger church became increasingly concerned about the drain of young adults away from institutional Christianity, Leadership sought to exercise its mission by helping to address the problem. Accordingly, it established what it called the Young Leaders Network, and in 1997 employed a thirtysomething named Doug Pagitt to head it. To speak in clichés, the rest was history. Pagitt was to become a major pastor and leader in Emergent Church and, thereby, in the larger construct of Emergence Christianity itself.

By 2000, Pagitt knew that what he was dealing with, while it might still be amorphous, was nonetheless on its way to taking shape and form. He knew as well that his job was not with Young Leaders Network so much as it was with what was rising up around him. His call was to this new branch of Christianity, not to the service of an extant one.

Emergent Church

One of the more droll stories coming out of the history of Emergence is one Pagitt tells about what he calls "that fateful day," and that most observers would now call an auspicious moment. It was the summer of 2000. Pagitt and some dozen or so friends, all of whom were by then involved in emerging church, were on a conference call. Pagitt was talking from his home in Minneapolis, and Brian McLaren, who is now recognized as the Martin Luther of Emergence internationally, was in Pagitt's living room on an extension line. Participating from other spots around the country were other movement leaders, men and women like Tony Jones, who would become the Theologian-in-Residence at Solomon's Porch and an intellectual force within Emergence; Tim Keel, founding pastor of Jacob's Well in Kansas City; Ivy Beckwith, authority on religious education for children and now on Emergence formation; Chris Seay, founding pastor of Ecclesias in Houston; Tim Conder, founding pastor of Emmaus Way in Durham, etc. In sum, the list seems now like a kind of roll call of Emergence heroes, but it was the purpose of the call that mattered.

For some thirty-plus years, "emerging church" had served as the popular name for what had been more a collection of attitudes and shared sensibilities than it was a construct, more a conversation itself than a plan, so to speak. But by 2000, some alignments and realignments had begun to happen within that larger conversation. Varying areas of shared proclivities and vocation had begun to coalesce and distinguish themselves, one from another. The conference call from Pagitt's house had been set up for the express purpose of trying to define and then clearly name what it was that the participants actually were.

As Pagitt's retelling of the story goes, the conversation was going nowhere until, out of weariness, the whole thing wandered off—providentially, most would say—to forestry, which clearly had nothing to do with the problem at hand. Or it didn't until someone began to talk about how treetops may look healthy from above, but the real future of a forest depends on the growth that's happening down below on the ground where the emergent growth is . . .

Bingo!

And then, someone else added, even forests that have no old growth can still have a rich future in their emergent growth . . .

Bingo again!

A day or two after the phone conference, it seemed wise to establish publicly the existence of Emergent Church as a self-aware entity within the larger conversation.[2] Setting up a website was the logical next step in that direction. Unfortunately, however, www.emergent.com already existed as a website for some other kind of group. Then providence struck again. Tim Keel suggested adding the idea of "village" to their thinking. Village, as in "it takes a village to raise a child," was what Emergent groups should emulate in their self-perception, and it certainly was the way the overarching, larger body of conversationalists should think of themselves. Emergent Village was born, though it was destined always to exist not as a place or an organizationally bound North American body within Emergence Christianity but as a website.[3]

Emergent Village

This website, www.emergentvillage.com, is as near a center or headquarters or home base as there is likely ever to be for Emergent

Christians, but it is also an unceasing, essentially uninterrupted conversation where ideas are posted and theology is argued and business is conducted. Some of the keenest minds and most influential Emergence Christian theologians and ecclesial leaders engage each other there in transparent, open-to-all discussions of what the faith is and how best to live it out in the twenty-first-century world.

An even more pivotal year for Emergence Christianity as a larger whole turned out to be 2004. Two things happened, both of them in the world of books. In 2001, Brian McLaren had written a conversation-generating book entitled *A New Kind of Christian*. As a result of that publication, he was already recognized internationally as a gifted theologian, lecturer, and teacher. Then, in 2004, McLaren released another book. This one was destined to become the Emergence analog of Martin Luther's Ninety-Five Theses on the door of Wittenberg church.

The book was *A Generous Orthodoxy*, but it is its full title that tells the tale. The full title is *A Generous Orthodoxy: Why I Am a missional, evangelical, post/protestant, liberal/conservative, mystical/poetic, biblical, charismatic/contemplative, fundamentalist/calvinist, anabaptist/anglican, catholic, green, incarnational, depressed-yet-hopeful, emergent, unfinished Christian*.[4] The whole world now not only knew what Emergence Christianity was but also and at last had a free fall of words by which to describe it.

One of the most pertinent stories about *A Generous Orthodoxy* has to do, though, not with McLaren or the US, but with the archbishop of Canterbury and the world in general. The story—whether an ecclesial myth or otherwise—goes that the archbishop, Rowan Williams, was on an airplane when he read *Orthodoxy* and that he said, once he had finished reading, that all he really wanted to do was buy up all the available copies of the book, hire a fleet of airplanes, and air-drop those copies all over the United Kingdom. Because, he is reported as having said, "This is what my people need to know, for God is indeed doing a new thing among us."

Air-dropping books did not prove to be practical, nor can anyone really believe the Archbishop truly meant to attempt such. Instead, being a practical man, he did a practical thing. He went back to Lambeth Palace, the center or Vatican of Anglicanism, and threw his insights and energies into furthering the newly established the Office of Fresh Expressions. And therein, as the storytellers are fond of saying, lieth the rest of the tale of the year of our Lord, 2004.

NOTES

1. Taken from "Emerging Church Movement (1989–2009)" as available on 12/30/09 at http://tallskinnykiwi.typepad.com/tallskinnykiwi/2009/12/emerging-church-movement-1989---2009.html. It is difficult to overstate Jones's contribution to the Emergence Christianity conversation internationally. A Brit based in the Orkney Islands, Jones writes under the rubric of Tall Skinny Kiwi, and anyone having serious interest in Emergence and its evolution since 1990 would be wise to avail himself or herself of Jones's postings.

2. Part of the appeal of this story and of the action whose history it recalls is that none of the conference call participants had read Metz's earlier work or, if they had, they did not recall it. Nor were any of them aware of Kalt and Wilkins or particularly concerned with Emergence Theory per se. Rather, they recognized this new naming as resonant with the current conversation but also as distinguishable from it. They liked as well the fact that "Emergent" kept the sense of action and ongoing change patent in "Emerging." The truth of the thing, though, Pagitt says, is that they got into the whole forestry conversation by way of complaining first to each other about pre-emergent herbicides. It was summer, after all, and their conversation was going nowhere—at least not at that point.

3. This does not mean, however, that Emergent Village is formless as well as placeless. There has been a very active board and an equally active chairman of the board from Village's earliest days. There is just not a hierarchy, either actual or implied, in how matters are considered and eventually decided. It must be added, however, that some four or five years into things, the board suffered a brief decline into former ways and decided there did need to be at least some modicum of administrative structure. Accordingly, Tony Jones was appointed as executive director. The whole thing lasted about thirteen months before all concerned agreed with Jones's declaration: "This isn't who we are or how we operate." The experiment ended, never to be tried again, at least not in any kind of top-down way.

4. Published by Zondervan as a Youth Specialties Book.

Part 3

Pulling Together

Defining What It Is and What It Is Not

13

Reporting on the Action

Documenting the Changes as They Happened

From the point of view of Emergence Christian history, there were two major publications in 2004. One was McLaren's *A Generous Orthodoxy*. The other was, at first blush, far less promising. It was, of all things, a report written by a committee.[1] Even more daunting, in terms of potential sales and readership, the committee was, as the frontispiece of the volume says, "a working group of the Church of England's Mission and Public Affairs Council," the chair of which was a bishop even: Graham Cray, Bishop of Maidstone, to be precise. More deadly than that could hardly be imagined, except . . .

. . . except that the book sold thousands of copies, has been reprinted, revised, and updated several times, has generated a good half-dozen spin-off volumes, and continues to sell well today. Its title is humble in both words and in typeface—*mission-shaped church*—but once again it is the subtitle that holds the secret. That subtitle is *church planting and fresh expressions of church in a changing context*. To some extent, it also was, and is, the bishop who held the secret. Bishop Cray knew what he was looking at. He was, in fact, an Emergence Christian in a bishop's mitre.

Fresh Expressions

The report called *mission-shaped church* was a clear-eyed, no-holds-barred assessment of what was happening in established church, but it also honored—and urged upon all Anglicans the honoring of—what Cray's committee called "Fresh Expressions of Church." That name would stick. Like Emergent Village and Emergent Church, Fresh Expressions would emerge, within a matter of two or three years, as an international subset within Emergence Christianity.

In his rather impassioned introduction to *mission-shaped church*, Bishop Cray argued that there could no longer be a standard form of church. Contextualization, he wrote, has a time-honored presence within the historic church's history, just not in the history of the Western church. It was time for that to change. Geography was no longer the defining raison d'être for a church. Rather, affinities and context were, and churches must be planted, as a result, not cloned. There must be networks of groups surrounding a parish (the kirk and chicks pattern, though he did not use that phrase). There would be a resulting "mixed-economy" of parish and extended network, moving together to serve and be the people of God in this place and in this time. An Emergence Christian in a bishop's mitre, indeed.

There was far more than passion and invigorating rhetoric in *mission-shaped church*, though. The Committee Report took the position that Christendom was dead, a stance that few other church groups had even been willing to mention, much less discuss.[2] Thus, the pages that followed the bishop's opening salvo are an analysis without apology of where established church, as it had existed within a Christendom system and context, now is, of where it has to go in order to do God's work outside of the comfort of establishment, and of how it is to get there.

The Un-Churched, the Non-Churched, and the De-Churched

The committee, in its report, repeatedly makes clear their belief that the mission-shaped church is called to those twenty-first-century men and women who live outside of Christianity, even as they also exist in a political and social context that no longer invites them to be even cultural Christians, much less practicing ones.

In explicating a mission-shaped church's approach to this, the report offers a nuanced taxonomy that has since become a part of the Emergence conversation wherever it happens. The mission field, says *mission-shaped*, is among the non-churched, the de-churched, and the un-churched. The approach to each is distinct, because the categories are distinct.

The un-churched are, as their name implies, more or less totally neutral on the subject of Christianity. They neither remember having been exposed to Christianity and/or its teachings and stories, nor do they remember holding any animosity toward it. The non-churched are those Christians, usually urban, who claim the faith nominally—or even sometimes a bit more actively—but who, for whatever reason, have not yet gotten around to the business of being connected in any way to Christian community, worship, or even praxis. It is not that they are not Christian, in other words; it is just that being or not being is of little practical consequence. The de-churched are those whose numbers are sizable and perhaps even growing. They are those who, having once been Christian to some greater or lesser extent, have been so offended by the Christianity they have known as to eschew it completely. This, then, says the committee's report, is where the mission field of today is.

As it turns out, the timing of the archbishop's reading of *A Generous Orthodoxy* and the release of *mission-shaped*, with its innovative analyses and proposals, was, like Doug Pagitt's meandering conference call, providential. That is, when the archbishop of Canterbury, unable to hire his fleet of airplanes, had gone back to Lambeth Palace instead and established the Office of Fresh Expressions, he based its remit to a large extent on the premises contained in *mission-shaped*.

From the very beginning, the Methodist Church in the United Kingdom joined the Church of England in the management, staffing, and funding of Fresh Expressions. By 2010, the Congregational Church and the United Reformed Church in England had also come to be participants, though in a more occasional way. In addition, several other churches internationally are now associated with Fresh Expressions programs and the Lambeth office.

Getting a Birth Certificate

Though 2004 had, indeed, been a good year, 2005 would also be kind, once again in terms of a book. In 2005, Dr. Eddie Gibbs, who is the Donald A. McGavran Professor of Church Growth at Fuller Theological Seminary, and Dr. Ryan Bolger, assistant professor of Church in Contemporary Culture and academic director of the master's program in Global Leadership at Fuller, published a book entitled *Emerging Churches: Creating Christian Community in Postmodern Cultures*.[3]

As a book, *Emerging Churches* would prove to be invaluable as a source for anyone wishing to know where the major sites of Emergence practice in North America are and who their leaders are. It is replete with commentary from those leaders and with information about where to contact them, just as it also is replete with insights about what emerging church is and why. That would have been more than sufficient reason for a book, but *Emerging Churches* was something more than that. It was the first book-length treatment by impartial, credentialed academics of what emerging church was and is.

As such, it was, in effect, a birth certificate. There was no way now for anyone to naysay what had been duly recorded.

NOTES

1. Published originally by Church House Publishing, London.
2. *mission-shaped church*, 84ff.
3. Published by Baker Books, Grand Rapids.

14

It Takes a Village . . .

The years since 2005 have been easier for Emergence Christians in some ways. They no longer have to explain themselves so frequently, much less defend themselves so constantly, to family and friends concerned about where they worship and why they live the way they do. The words "Emergence Christianity" no longer elicit a quizzical look or, even worse, a contemptuous snort. The blogosphere is full of energetic Emergence conversation, and even mainstream media pay kindly inclined attention to the whole thing. But if birth certificates and greater acceptance are sweet, they also can be seductive. They can dull the edge, steal the alertness, dampen the urgency. When one has walked into the wind for a long period, having the wind abruptly die is less a blessing than an invitation to stumble. Changing from a bent-forward, head-down position to one of walking upright and normally takes a moment or two. For Emergence, it actually took a year or two.

By 2009, enough once-ardent Emergences had begun to withdraw themselves from active conversations and blog exchanges that, sotto voce, some observers were beginning to wonder whether or not they had been mistaken. Would the current Emergence Christian responses to the Great Emergence prove themselves to have been no more than ecclesial will-o'-the-wisps? Was this it, or were we to wait for another, after all?

Even the Tall Skinny Kiwi, Anthony Jones, asked publicly if 2009 was to be the end of the Emergent ethos. He kicked up a huge dust storm when he did that, of course, proving that there was more life in the beast than he had thought. (Proving also, we should add, that greater discretion in the future about what one chooses to kick might be a good idea.) Yet even *World* magazine, a respected Christian news magazine, opened 2010 with a post reading, "Farewell, Emerging Church." But only twelve months later, things were very different.

A State of Emergence

Jonathan Brink would be a force to be reckoned with in any context. He is a leader in TransFORM, a missional-church body within the ethos of Emergence Christianity, as well as an author and speaker of insight and skill. More to the point here, however, is the fact that, commencing in 2009, Brink began to post, through www.emergentvillage.com, annual reports entitled "A State of Emergence." In these reports, Brink essentially chronicles the major events of the previous year and projects, based on them, what the coming year might reasonably be expected to do and/or become. In his "State of Emergence 2010," which he posted in January of 2011, Brink summed the preceding twenty-four months by saying:

> In many ways this public declaration of death was needed. What arguably died was a perception of the slick marketing model aimed at middle class, white, hipsters saddled in the corner of Starbucks with their Macs. This stereotype has run its course and run out of

> favor. It had to die. What didn't die were the underlying questions that fueled the movement in the first place. People were still gathering together in pubs, coffee houses, and homes, wrestling with questions of faith, reformation, atonement, the goodness of God, what it means to follow Jesus, and how to live in a post-Christian culture.[1]

Brink was correct, of course. Emergence Christianity had not died, but it had shed a deceptive and destructive public persona. It had shed as well, at least to some extent, most of those restless souls who had only been passing through Emergence on their way to the next coolest thing. Brink's summary serves as a kind of R.I.P. for them, certainly, but basically it remains as an impassioned call to authentic Christian existence for those who have chosen to live on toward Emergence's full maturing.

With Brink's words of benediction and exhortation, we can bring our summary excursion into Emergence Christianity's history to an end. Now we must assume Brink's posture of first describing what currently is and then, working from that, of trying to diagnose in a practical and useful way what is becoming. Before we do that, though, one last thing must be said. It must be said, because it is too poignant to be left unsaid—or it was poignant beyond saying to Emergence Christian leaders in mid-2009 when the premature news of their death was swirling about them and becoming almost credible, even to them.

Being Recognized

The *Handbook of Denominations* is a master-census of the various recognized Christian bodies functioning in North America. As a highly respected reference work, it chronicles the doctrines and polity of such bodies. It is also probably as near to objective, neutral credentialing as Christian ecclesial bodies ever get in this country.

To be in the *Handbook* is to be declared "real" within the reality of the church-at-large.

Because of its importance and its very substantial usefulness, the *Handbook* is updated on a regular basis, and the 2010 edition included, for the first time, a presentation of Emergence under the listing of Emergent Village.

By the time the 2010 edition actually published, the brouhaha of Emergence's moribund status and impending death had already begun to subside. It was not, then, so much the release of the registry that was sweet. What was sweet had happened several months earlier in June of 2009 when word of the pending inclusion had come from the *Handbook*'s editor to Emergent Village. To be affirmed is always pleasant, but to be affirmed while in extremis is joy almost beyond all bounds.

Beyond the sweet balm of recognition, however, there was one other part of the *Handbook*'s announcement of intention to include that was equally significant, just not as immediately satisfying. In his note of intention, the editor wrote that, because of limited space, the 2010 edition "will have to cover the entire Emergent movement with the Emergent Village entry." He went on, though, to acknowledge his editorial board's awareness of other "emergent (or emerging) churches" and of the need to include them in later editions.[2]

NOTES

1. The material quoted here is available at http://www.emergentvillage.com/weblog/brink-state-of-emergence-2010. Interested readers and students of current Emergence Christianity will, however, want to explore much more of what Brink has written, both on the web and in his books. Many of his columns not only convey information but are so penetrating as well that they elicit some of the liveliest reader comments and responses on the web. See, for example, http://www.emergentvillage.com/weblog/brinkdeathofemergence for an especially rich engagement of the issues raised in this chapter.

2. The correspondence occurred on June 17, 2009, between Deacon Atwood, editor of *Handbook*, and Tripp Fuller, an EV leader and prominent Emergence podcaster. It was immediately circulated on sites and blogs all over the web for obvious reasons and with great relish.

15

Distinguishing This from That

What Organizational Patterns Can Tell Us

Emergence Christianity is not a physical address or organization in the way that Roman Catholicism, Protestantism, Anglicanism, and Orthodoxy have accustomed us to think of "church" as being. Consequently, it is impossible either to define or to "locate" it in the ways or with the standard definitions that most of us are used to employing. What Emergence Christians do exhibit and what is describable, however, is a kind of "centrality of mind-set." The existence of that "mind-set" is a circumstance for which commentators and students of Emergence are routinely grateful. That cache of shared sensibilities, values, and positions is not only the best but more or less the only sensible and productive route into any kind of usable description of what Emergence really is.

Obviously, there is some danger in using this approach. When we speak of Emergence Christianity in a block and as if it were some kind of an unsegmented, undifferentiated whole, we immediately run into the risk of conflation and oversimplification.

There are as many variations on the themes we are about to look at as there are house churches, pub theology groups, web-based confraternities, and even individual Emergence Christians.[1] With that caveat in mind, however, it is entirely possible to make some very informing observations about what *is* in general, in order that we may more wisely engage, and more accurately project, what Emergence Christianity may do and come to be within the larger scope of Christianity over the next five hundred years.

Any cursory overview of the history of Emergence Christianity, especially in North America—and certainly a history like the one we have just finished—will produce a laundry list of most of Emergence Christianity's distinguishing concerns and attitudes just by bent of telling its story. For instance, even if nothing else were ever said, the subtitle of Brian McLaren's *A Generous Orthodoxy* alone provides a dozen or so of Emergence Christianity's attitudinal and theological postures all by itself. For our purposes here, though, it might be better to commence not so much with values and attitudes but with something more overt. That is, taking a look first at some of the organizational patterns of Emergence can, like McLaren's subtitle, be a tangible introduction to other and less tangible attitudes undergirding the whole.[2]

Inherited Church

Over the years since 2004 and the impact of *mission-shaped church* upon the general conversation, it has become good form to use the terminology of "inherited church" and "fresh expressions church" to distinguish between the established or institutional church and the one that is emerging.[3] One of the most telling differences between those two is that inherited church, because it is an institution and functions by the rules of institutional structure, measures itself in terms of numbers. That is, it gauges itself in terms of numbers of people joining and amounts of money collected. How many members and how big a budget are the prime and telling indices. Over the last fifty years of living in a media age, the institution has also come to measure itself to some extent by the amount of public visibility and, thereby, of influence it commands. All three of those concerns are so alien to fresh expressions or Emergence Church as to seem almost to be items from some kind of foreign-language vocabulary list.

Market success—for that is what self-measurement by size, budget, and public influence is trying to determine—is neither an Emergence concept nor even an Emergence virtue. Success in any fresh expression of church, when it enters the conversation at all, refers most usually to mechanical things like whether or not a service has been mounted on the web without a hitch or whether or not the distance teacher for a gathering has been Skyped in such a way that everybody could comfortably see, hear, and participate with him or her. Numerical counts, when they happen, will be more commentary than tally and more subjective than objective. The questions will be concerned with matters like whether a posting did or did not elicit a gratifying number of hits or with whether the presence of the Spirit was or was not corporately as well as individually perceived in a gathering. Even then, the concerns and observations are nearer to being an introspective assessment than any kind of implied basis for setting new and larger goals.[4]

Is Growth Necessary?

Another considerable part of the reason for the disparity in thinking between inherited church and fresh expressions church is that measuring by numbers, visibility, and influence presupposes, to some greater or lesser extent, a tomorrow that is not only more significant than today but that is also obligatory. Permanence, long-range planning, and longevity are virtues for any institution. They are burdens for Emergence, burdens whose maintenance ultimately and inevitably will become taskmasters, not to mention threatening impediments to the mobility and immediacy that are required if the kingdom of God is to be served on this earth.

Thus, a pub theology group may be deliberately started or, more likely, it may simply happen because the pub is, after all, a neighborhood pub and conducive to serious talk. As a group, this one may gather together a dozen people, or perhaps even three dozen people, all of whom are modestly curious about religion, or are royally annoyed with the Christianity they see around them and want a place to say so, or are looking for authentic Bible discussion with somebody else who truly cares as much. Or perhaps they simply are passionate about worship that is authentic. Or maybe they just seek the familiar company and sustained, personal prayer support of other devout Christians. Or maybe they are just somewhere in between all of those. Whatever they are, that group will become what the Spirit and the members make of it in prayer and participation. But at some point, it will do one of two or three things.

It may grow in such a way as not only to exceed the barkeep's tolerance but also—and more importantly—to exceed the psychology of a small group approach and, as a result, will need to become something nearer to a self-aware group. As such, it may—and probably will—go looking for space to rent where worship can be more candid and more liturgical and where others can more easily be included in the circle.

Or it may break apart. More accurately said, the original pub group will simply drift apart from one another in much the same way that a milkweed pod breaks open in the fall, sending dozens of its seed-laden parachutes out into the surrounding countryside. Where originally there had been one group in one pub, there now will be, as if by accident and certainly without announced intention, a clutch of three or four groups scattered around and about the area.

Or the group may just cease, period, end of story. It will have served its purpose, fed the Christian life of those who composed it, and will now become less than what they have grown to need. Friends will remain friends, and acquaintances, acquaintances, but it's time to move on.

It may safely be said here that institutions cannot even begin to think that way, and Emergences are categorically unable to think in any other way. It is a core difference that, superficial as it may sound at first, feathers out to impact almost every part of how the two differing bodies do the business of God.

People, Not Places

By default, if nothing else, Emergence automatically assumes—to borrow a cliché here—that "church" is a people to be, not a place to go. Given that more or less knee-jerk bias, the whole business of real estate or "place" is greatly simplified. If more space is needed than can be supplied by a pub or a home, then some other alternative must be found to rent. To buy is usually out of the question for the vast majority of Emergence cells or nodes, though not for financial reasons, at least not primarily. Rather, to buy would be to formalize themselves. To buy would be to knowingly set themselves dead center of a huge vat of financial and administrative cement. Not good. Not good at all.

Whatever is going to be rented (or bought, as does sometimes happen) must meet certain criteria. The principal one of these arises from a vigorous egalitarianism that is inherent in all Emergence, be it sacred or profane, as well as from an instinctual dedication to what Wimber labeled as center-set vs. bound-set ecclesiology. Whatever is to be used must be as open to all of humanity as, for example, a public park is. The homeless, the damaged, the ne'er-do-well, and the naïve are welcome, and they must be as comfortable as the nurse, the lawyer, the university student, and the cop.

In sum, whatever is occupied must be as impervious to damage and as user-friendly as an old bowling alley (which, by the way, the chosen space often is) or an old-timey movie house on a summer night.[5] The space can even be—and quite frequently is—a previously abandoned church building. We need to be very clear about that, for the leavings of the institutional church have considerable appeal to Emergence groups when those forsaken naves show up as spaces for rent but not for ownership.

Emergence Christians are instinctively liturgical. Webber's ancient-future is firmly planted in both their spiritual and their religious essence. And the truth is, it is hard to do a beautiful mass in an old bowling alley—hard, but not impossible.[6] Either way, though, it is much easier to do and experience a Celtic mass or a choral evensong when it is held in space that has, at least to some extent, been constructed for such exercises of worship.

Before we move any farther in this discussion of the physically demonstrable characteristics of Emergence, though, we should make note here of two other things. First, much of the appeal for Hyphenated Emergence Christians in their decision to remain within their natal tradition while seeking to infuse it with Emergence sensibilities is this very thing. Hyphenateds, by definition, have more or less ready access to consecrated space when they desire it. Second, one of the appeals of the kirk-and-chicks format finds its roots here also. As a modus operandi, that scattered approach allows inherited church congregations and fresh expressions church groups to interface with one another upon occasion with theological impunity and mutual spiritual benefit.[7] Ultimately, that proves to be a good thing from almost everybody's point of view.

Organized by Consensus

Not all the major hallmarks of Emergence organizational patterns show up, however, in a lack of concern for permanency or in sometimes-unusual choices of places to worship. Regardless of transience or the lack thereof and regardless of the type of space occupied, the internal dynamics are also distinctive, for whatever else they are, Emergence Christian gatherings most surely are self-organizing and self-correcting. They move communally and organize by consensus. Authority within any Emergence grouping is granted by the group itself rather than by any extrinsic authority, and always on a commutable basis. Likewise, authority is determined and described by the group in accord with perceived needs, not in accord with any externally established or habituated ways of doing church.

In part, this shift is due to the fact that, in an era of exponentially expanding information and of unprecedented, almost universal, access to most of it, there can be no such thing as an expert, at least not in the historic sense of that concept. Thus—the line of argument goes—an expert, if he or she exists at all, is one who understands some very small part of something well enough to make a meaningful contribution to a conversation vetted by other people who have engaged the same bit(s) of information with the same degree of informed intention. And if that sentence seems clotted, it does because it is.

What the overburdened sentence describes is the wiki approach that, once again, is part and parcel of Emergence, regardless of whether it is secular or profane. *Wikipedia* obviously got its name from this construct and still serves as its best-known example. In a wiki world, it is the group, and only the group, that can hope to reach around any subject at all. There is simply too much to know and to integrate into what is already known. At a practical level and from the point of view of religious practice, the loss of faith in the expert translates most immediately not only into the group's governing dynamics but also into a loss of faith in the pastor as the source of all knowledge and right interpretation.

This shift away from reverencing the pastor as head of the group brings with it a sincere hesitation about the wisdom of, let alone the need for, seminary education and/or externally validated ordination. Nor should these changes be seen as matters of disrespect. They are not. Rather, they are matters of common sense, as Emergence pastors themselves often are the first to acknowledge. Thus it is that, within Emergence, the lead pastor in a large group, or just the leader in a small one, is no more privileged than is any other member of the gathering. He or she occupies a function, not a status.

Doug Pagitt, in his principal role of lead pastor at Solomon's Porch in Minneapolis, probably offers the clearest summary of this difference when he says, "The ability to teach and preach and lead is taking a backseat to the pastor's capacity to create and facilitate open-source faith experiences for the people of the church."[8] The open-source part of Pagitt's statement is also central in another way to the shift in posture that he is describing. Everything is open-source for those of us alive and functioning in the Great Emergence, or at least it is at a practical level. The members of today's worshiping bodies, be they inherited or fresh expressions congregants, have immediate access through the web to more biblical criticism, more theological and church history, more astute exegesis, more fine exhortation, and more talking heads than any seminarian or seminary professor or ordained pastor of fifty years ago could ever have even hoped for. The truth in that lies, in no small part, in the fact that he or she would simply not have known, fifty years ago, that three-quarters to nine-tenths of said material was even in existence.

Open-source, just like everything else affecting religion, has its dangers, of course. Since no one can know of, much less comprehend, all that is available on websites, blogs, and our burgeoning social media, there inevitably will be a kind of capricious or unintentional selection process involved. Random or uninformed choices will often determine what is and is not seen or accessed.[9] For that reason, discernment—deeply practiced, communal discernment of everything offered in worship—is integral to Emergences' practice in a way that probably has not accrued since the first century and that certainly is unique to them in today's latinized Christianity.

In this regard, there are two matters that need a bit of expansion before we move on. The first of these is patent, certainly, in the word *discernment* and, therefore, probably wants emphasizing more than anything else.

Discernment

Lesslie Newbigin was, without a doubt, the great missiologist of the twentieth century, and his influence on Emergence Christianity in all its presentations has been enormous. Newbigin, by the 1950s, was saying to all who would listen that nobody, up to that time, had even begun to start to appreciate what the impact of Pentecostalism was going to be on Christianity in the years ahead.[10] He was, in this as in most of what he said, as accurate as a prophet as he was insightful as a missiologist.

Azusa Street—or at least what grew out from the Azusa Street coming of the Spirit—was not just about descending flames of fire and healings by miracle and speaking in tongues. It was about those things, certainly, but not principally. Principally, it was, and continues to be, about listening, about engaging corporately and individually the presence and instruction of the Holy Spirit. It was and is about discernment and, then, about obedience to what had been given during that process. Emergence Christianity today is governed, first and foremost, by this kind of discernment among the gathered. Governance in Emergence, consequently, is always going to be just beyond the reach of titles and addresses and location, but it is definitely going to be operative and directed.

Ordained Clergy

The second thing that does need brief expansion here has to do with the business of ordained clergy as it operates within and/or in relation to many small pods and hyphenated groups within Emergence Christianity. The distancing of fresh expressions church from seeking the oversight of seminary-trained and institutionally ordained clergy is not, as we have already said, one of animosity. It is, rather and as we have also noted, twofold. It fears that academic theology, most of which still comes almost entirely out of the institutional church, will indoctrinate and thereby limit the seminarian as pastor; and second, it regards the proper clerical role as a much humbler thing than once it was. That kind of posture is sustainable, in both large and small groups, where the explication and study of Scripture are concerned, for instance, or where the business of determining liturgy and praxis and even basic ecclesiology are the issues. In smaller groups or hyphenated ones where there is no ordained presence of any sort known, it is not so sustainable emotionally—or even legally—where marriage, infant baptism, and burial are concerned. For many Emergences, especially Hyphenateds, it is not even sustainable where the consecration of the elements for the Eucharist is concerned.

Most small Emergence groups—house churches, nodes, pods, cohorts, whatever—could not offer any kind of financial support to an ordained clergyperson, even if they wanted one. They are too few in number for that. Yet, to provide for the inevitable events in life like marriage, baptism, burial, and consecration, they too need and want an ordained person who is not just "some collar available at the moment for a fee." No, what they want is someone who is a known and consistent spiritual friend. Maybe—ideally!—even one who is a member of their group, but only as a member and as a fellow Christian. Or, barring that, maybe someone who comes in and out of the group's gatherings on a consistent, but not programmed, basis. What they want is what inherited church has long known and some dismissively labeled as tentmakers or the diaconate or bi-vocational clergypersons.

Perhaps no single entity within all of the physical evidences of Emergence Christian Church and its impact on inherited church has proved to be quite so just plain intriguing as has this one. Certainly, none has caused more conversation and elicited more passion from the segment of the clergy involved.

Established church, in all its forms, has never been consistently clear about what its diaconate can and cannot do. Most bodies, of course, do recognize that whatever it is, the diaconate is certainly credentialed in some way beyond that of the laity, just as it is given license to officiate over some things not permitted to lay execution. Likewise, every segment of inherited church has always been a bit ambivalent about bi-vocational pastors, those men and women who colloquially refer to themselves as self-supporting clergy. Following in the footsteps of the apostle Paul, they have been called not to congregationally supported ministry but to exercising a clerical presence and ministry within the secular workplace where they also earn their own livelihood. Theirs is a much looser, usually less assigned or permanent ministry, and nothing, absolutely nothing, could be better suited to the needs of Emergence Christians. More important, nothing could be more appealing to hundreds of deacons and tentmakers than are those fresh expressions groups.

When one attempts to project the near future of both established church and Emergence Church, one of the first things that will have to be considered is exactly how the expanding role and participation of the diaconate and the company of tentmakers will affect both bodies. Conceivably, the most open and feasible route of communication between the two may lie just here, with those who by choice and vocation walk back and forth between the two camps.

NOTES

1. One of the wittiest and most engaging explications of this conundrum was written in 2010 by Professor William Brosend, director of the Advanced Degrees Program for the School of Theology at Seewanee: the University of the South. In an article titled "Discerning the Emergent Church," he cautions: "There is no limited or limiting way of being emergent, and while there are some ways of being and doing church that are perhaps *not* emergent, anyone who says, 'This is emergent and that is not,' probably needs to travel more" (*Sewanee Magazine*, fall 2010, p. 33).

2. There is, in this regard, another subtitle that rivals McLaren's and speaks directly to overt patterns with the same acuity that McLaren's speaks to attitudes and stances. Kester Brewin, a Londoner, is a major figure in Emergence internationally, the administrative head of the annual Greenbelt Festival, and a commanding presence in the Emergence blogosphere. In 2004, he published with the British house SPCK a volume entitled *The Complex Christ: Signs of Emergence in the Urban Church*. The book was—and remains—highly influential, and in 2007 was released in a US edition by Baker Publishing Group. But by 2007, the title had become *Signs of Emergence: A Vision for Church That Is Organic/Networked/Decentralized/Bottom-up/Communal/Flexible {Always Evolving}*, a change that reveals even more than it says.

3. This movement away from "success" concepts and their definition by numbers, while it is a dominant characteristic now, was less true prior to the 2009 year of crisis and self-criticism for Emergence. It still continues today to be less true of some mega or more evangelical gatherings within Emergence, especially of those who speak of themselves as "emerging" churches.

4. A word of caution here about terminology. There is a kind of maddening difference between *fresh expressions* and *Fresh Expressions*. The lowercased one is the only name we really have so far for speaking of all presentations of Emergence Church in aggregate. The uppercased one is a distinct division within Emergence Christianity. Maddening indeed, as well as unfortunate and confusing.

5. The most biblical explanation of this that I had seen in a very long time came in 2011 from Mark Batterson, lead pastor of National Community Church in Washington, DC. In explaining why National had bought an old 1930s-style movie house in the Barrack's Row area of Capitol Hill, Pastor Batterson told reporters, "We like doing business in marketplace environments similar to how Jesus hung out at the well. Coffee houses are like postmodern wells and movie theatres are like the Aeropagus [sic]" ("DC Church Turns Owner of Historic Movie House," *Religion Today Summaries*, Crosswalk.com, June 9, 2011, http://www.crosswalk.com/news/religiontoday-news-summaries/religion-today-summaries-june-9-2011.html).

6. On a purely personal note, I must say here that one of the most effectually moving and deeply sacred Eucharists I have ever attended was in worshiping some years ago with the Birmingham, Alabama, Emergence cohort in an old bowling alley on the fringe of Birmingham's downtown. The whole experience was Bishop Spong's catacombs church in every sense of that analogy, and I shall go to my grave grateful for having been welcomed into it.

7. Emergence leaders in both the UK and the US have been increasingly articulate about the interplay between sacramental tradition and sacred space. In particular, one thinks immediately of Ian Mobsby of Moot and Richard Giles of Liturgyworks in the United Kingdom and, in the United States, of Karen Ward, founding pastor of Church of the Apostles, and Nadia Bolz-Weber of House for All Sinners and Saints. An excellent introduction to the depth and scope of the discussion can be found in *Fresh Expressions in the Sacramental Tradition* as listed in the annotated bibliography in this volume.

8. *Church in the Inventive Age* (Sparkhouse/Augsburg Fortress, 2010), 33.

9. It should be noted here, however, that an increasing number of websites, both inherited and fresh expressions ones, seek to aggregate lists of and/or selections from other websites and web-based sources that might be of use to the study of specific areas within Christian theology and praxis. For fresh expressions groups, the prime example of this is the Faith Collaboratory, a joint effort of the Emerging Christian Way Media Society and Emergent Village. See www.faithcollaboratory.com, www.ecwmedia.org, and www.emergentvillage.org, respectively.

10. Paul Weston, a Newbigin scholar, has put together a rich compilation of Newbigin's writings (*Lesslie Newbigin: Missionary Theologian: A Reader* [Eerdmans, 2006]) in which these ideas are presented in Newbigin's own words and at some length. See the annotated bibliography in this volume.

Emergence Christianity

The Photographic Report

The Shirt Says It All

A CENTRAL CHARACTERISTIC or principle of Emergence Christianity is its aggressive belief in inclusivity and the importance of diversity in worship and in community. This person, captured by the camera while attending an Emergence gathering, has decided to wear that message as well as follow it.

The first view here—that of the community as it is gathering—reflects the informality, sociability, and joie de vivre of most Emergence praxis. Typical as well is the earnestness and fixed attention to the Word, shown in the second photograph.

Worship Service at Solomon's Porch—Minneapolis

Worship Service at Solomon's Porch—Minneapolis

Solomon's Porch-ers regard themselves as twenty-first-century Christians in every way, even dating the Porch from its inaugural service on the first Sunday of 2000. Like most Emergence communities, SP is leery of owning real estate and/or of real estate that is too pristine and well-appointed. Accordingly, the community worships, as seen here, in an old, abandoned Lutheran building which they rent and which, as one can see, they have reconfigured and reappointed to accommodate Emergence aesthetics, liturgy, and values.

ncarnating the Word through Art

n EMERGENCE PRACTICE, the word *incarnate* takes on an added theological neaning. Not only does it continue to refer to the assumption of human flesh y God in the person of Jesus, but it also refers to the imperative that the ody be used as a vehicle of worship and of receiving into itself physically he Word as it is spoken and revealed in worship. Thus it is quite usual to see vorshipers engaged in translating what they are hearing and experiencing nto a physical or tangible form. Sometimes, as here, the translation process s two-dimensional visual art. Sometimes it is three-dimensional, sometimes lance, sometimes meditation, etc. In each case, though, the thrust is always oward "embodying" the faith.

The so-called Hyphenateds are Emergence Christians who, despite being fully "emergence" in sensibilities and character, do not wish to lay aside completely the praxis and traditions of their natal denominations or communions. One of the "wild cards" or "X-factors" in Emergence Christianity, in fact, is the growing numbers of Hyphenateds and their concomitantly increasing influence upon the larger body of Emergence thought.

Before Worship Begins

The House for All Sinners and Saints in Denver is a luthermergent bod or, put another way, an example of luthermergence in the US. It evidence all the characteristic concerns and practices of Emergence (cf. p. P-5, Bless ing of the Bicycles; and p. P-12, Chocolate after Easter Vigil). But it als retains a great deal of traditional Lutheran form in its worship as well as strong sense of the need for transcendence and an abiding emphasis upo contemplative prayer. Caught in this candid shot by a HFASS congregant the community's pastor, Nadia Bolz-Weber, gathers her soul to enter an lead HFASS's worship. The shot, in and of itself, is iconic, speaking, as does, the truth of all Hyphenateds.

A NOTEWORTHY CONCERN in Emergence Christian praxis is the need to sacramentalize urban experiences in the same way that older forms of the faith traditionally have sacramentalized the pieces, parts, and events of rural experience. The Blessing of the Bicycles at the House for All Sinners and Saints in Denver, Colorado, is a case in point.

Announcing the Blessing of the Bicycles

BEGUN IN 1970 in San Francisco by two Episcopalian priests, St. Greg's, as it is known, is the oldest anglimergent congregation in the United States. While no photograph can adequately convey the Eucharistic joy of communion at St. Greg's, this one captures at least some of the strong sense of community that abides among the communicants. It captures as well, for the careful observer, the incorporation into St. Gregory's praxis of Eastern and Oriental Orthodox traditions and appointment, often a hallmark of Emergence worship (cf. p. P-12 of chocolate at Easter).

Celebrating the Eucharist at St. Gregory's

Because of St. Gregory's relatively long history, it exhibits some charac teristics that may or may not prove to be predictive of the course of other younger Emergence groups. The congregation, for example, owns its owr building. It, in this century, has assumed formal ties with the larger Church It also has, as shown here, some of the most sophisticated and sensitiv humanitarian relief programs in US Christendom. The Food Pantry at St Greg's is famous far beyond San Francisco.

Photo by David Sanger

Friday Is Food Pantry Day

Every Friday afternoon, parishioners gather to dispense nine tons of fresh vegetables, breads, meats, etc., to fifteen hundred people. Shown here is the beginning of the cleanup from a recent Friday's Pantry. What is not shown are the wandering musicians and/or accordionist who entertain the patrons of the Pantry while they "shop" the various tables for their food. Not shown either are the fresh-cut flowers sometimes available for Pantry patrons to take home with their groceries. Perhaps most telling of all, though, is the fact that if one looks closely, one will realize that the food tables and stalls are in sacred space. That is, the space shown here is exactly the same as the space shown above in the Eucharistic scene.

THE BUFFALO COMMUNITY of the Holy Spirit is either unique among Emergence and Hyphenated Emergence groups or it is a predictor of things to come. No one is quite sure just yet.

Meeting weekly in a once-abandoned and now-reclaimed office building in downtown Buffalo, Holy Spirit looks like just another Hyphenated community of some three dozen folk. In this shot, their priest, Ellen Brauza+, likewise looks like any other liturgical officiant as she consecrates the elements at the Community's regular Tuesday evening Eucharist. What is unusual are two stipulations in the Community's Rule of Life, the first two pages of which follow here. (The Rule may be seen in its entirety at http://holyspiritbuffalo.org/who-we-are/rule-of-life/.)

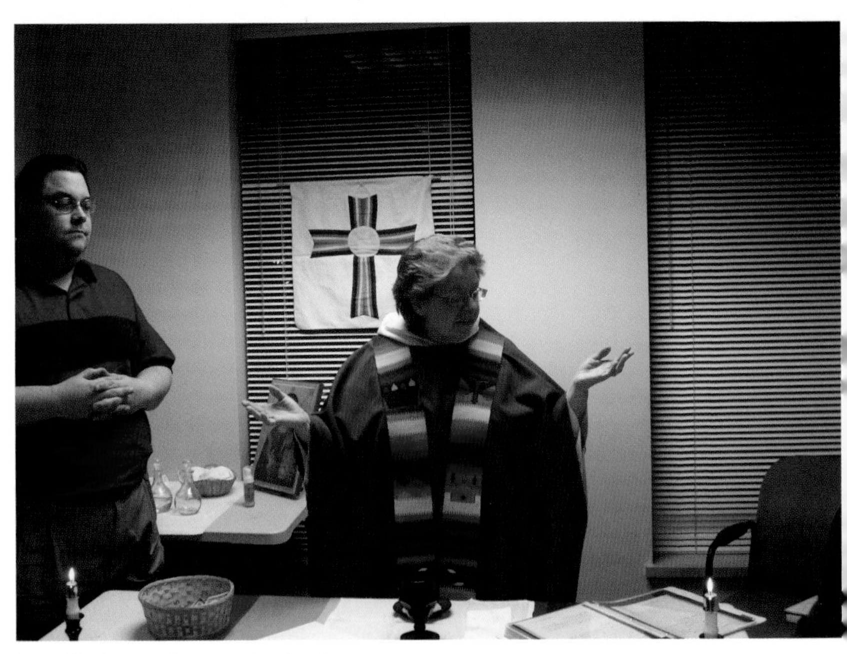

Rev. Ellen Brauza Consecrating the Elements

Even the casual observer can scan the Buffalo Rule and see that, paragraph by paragraph, it lists in very clear language most of the governing principles, prejudices, and tenets of Emergence praxis. What is unique here—and highlighted in yellow—is the pledge by each member of the Buffalo Community to remain an active and present part of his or her own denominational congregation as well as—and as part of—being a vowed member of the Community. This swearing of effectual allegiance to the inherited church, even while serving in and being vowed into a fresh expression of church, is an act of grace and inspired direction, wherever it may ultimately lead or not lead other such communities.

Our Rule of Life

Come, Holy Spirit, come. Come as the fire and burn. Come as the wind and cleanse. Convict, convert, consecrate, 'til we are wholly yours.

Who we are

Buffalo Community of the Holy Spirit is a non-residential, intentional Christian Community. We strive, in our common life, to model God as we have seen him revealed in Jesus.

We are first and foremost baptized Christians. Most of us are Episcopalians, and we joyfully accept the authority and fellowship of the Bishop of Western New York. Membership in the Community nevertheless remains open to any Christian who so desires.

In a time when many political and religious voices assert the claims of the nuclear family, we witness to Jesus' example of the intentional family of his followers. "Whoever does the will of God is my brother and sister and mother." (Mark 3:35) We function as a family, united by ties of faith and love. Some of us are single; others are married or in committed relationships.

In a time when both Church and society are all too often divided by race, class, gender, sexual orientation, or by human perceptions of rig
healed and fed both gentile
with them." (Luke 15:2) Our

In a time when property is o
places and buildings, we wi
itinerant ministry of Jesus. "
nowhere to lay his head." (M
worship wherever we are we

In a time when religious insti
sacrificial love of Jesus. "...
something to be exploited, b

We take our ministry of pres
we are. We keep our own ne
majority of our common fund
may be temporary, and hold
Spirit.

In a time when power and p
equality Jesus asked of his
(Mark 9:35) We recognize on

Worship

We commit ourselves as a Community to a weekly celebration of the Eucharist, (or, when necessary, of Evening Prayer,) and we pledge ourselves individually to attend that celebration faithfully, insofar as we are able. We further commit ourselves to participate fully in the worship life of the particular parishes and congregations of which we may be members.

We commit ourselves to some regular observance of the Daily Office, wherever we may be, as adapted to our individual circumstances. Minimally, the Lord's Prayer and the Community Prayer may suffice in cases of necessity.

We commit ourselves to a ministry of intercession, by praying the Anglican Rosary according to our Community custom, each week on our appointed day, for the needs and intentions of the larger community, as represented on the Community's prayer list.

Doctrine

We commit to ongoing discussion, as a Community, of our understanding of Scripture and contemporary life in the light of holy Tradition.

We commit ourselves to the best use of Reason of which we are capable in all our reading, learning, and discussion.

Action

We commit ourselves to the faithful support, according to our means, of the congregations and parishes of which we may be members, and to the support of the needs, work, and service projects of the Community, insofar as we are able. We commit ourselves to bear witness to the Gospel at all times, wherever we may be, through our actions and our words, and recognize the presence of God in everyone we meet. We commit ourselves to service to the larger community, and to bring the needs of others to the attention of the Community as we learn of them.

Structure and governance

We recognize and honour the gifts of everyone and the equality of all. At the same time, we recognize the need for certain roles and functions within the Community for the sake of order.

The Community's pastor shall be a priest in good standing, and shall be responsible for the celebration of the Eucharist, the distribution of other liturgical duties, the keeping of proper sacramental records, and shall be accountable both to the Community and to the Bishop.

The Community shall designate a treasurer to have custody of the Community's funds and bank account, to provide regular accounting of such funds, and to make dispersal as the Community decides and directs. In the event we are led to disband, whatever funds or possessions the Community may have shall be given to the Diocese of Western New York, with the hope that these may continue to be used to enhance ministry to the GLBT community.

The Community's governing body shall be the chapter, which shall consist of all members who are currently subscribed to this Rule. All shall have equal voice. The needs of the entire Community, as well as of the

Courtesy of Buffalo Community of the Holy Spirit

Altar Arrangement at a Mishkhah Service

An expanding presentation of Emergence Christianity is that of Alt Worship. Originally known as Alternative Worship and now shortened to Alt, the term names communities and services that occur in traditional church structures and/or are attached, to some greater or lesser extent, to established congregations or parishes.

For a traditional congregation that has a growing number of Emergence congregants among their own numbers and/or potential congregants in their surrounding neighborhoods, knowing how to create Emergence/Alt worship is neither self-evident nor easy to accomplish. Accordingly, two or three entrepreneurial organizations have sprung up, offering assistance. That assistance can run the gamut from simple counsel to providing music and appropriate liturgical suggestions to importing and conducting complete services on site. One vibrant and highly effective example of this phenomenon is Mishkhah.

Shown here is the chancel of St. John's Cathedral in Denver during a Mishkhah service. Also shown in close-up is a station table prepared for the same service.

A strong sense of the primal informs much of Emergence worship. In this, Emergence shows a clear affinity with Celtic sensibilities. As a result, the placement of naturally occurring artifacts—in this case, water-smooted stones—is often a part of worship and prayer space.

Photo by Elizabeth Harlan/Mishkhah worship creations courtesy of Katie Eaton

Cathedral Chancel Dressed for a Mishkhah Service

Emergence Christianity borrows heavily from both Orthodox and Anglican liturgical traditions. Particularly, in the case of Orthodoxy, we see this pattern in the escalating use of icons in Emergence worship space or in increasing familiarity with many of the early Fathers of the Church. Sometimes, however, the borrowing becomes more playful and/or definitely charming.

Courtesy of Amy Clifford

Chocolate after Easter Vigil

Chocolate is deeply entwined in Orthodox observance, being especially identified with Easter and resurrection. Forbidden during Lent and other fasts, it is joyfully received as part of the Easter celebration. While some Emergence groups go so far as to include chocolate in all Eucharistic celebrations as a third element along with the bread and wine, it is more common to see it simply incorporated into Easter festivities per se. Here, worshipers end the Easter Vigil at House for All Sinners and Saints with rejoicing . . . and, of course, with chocolate. According to HFASS's pastor, Nadia Bolz-Weber, "Nothing says 'resurrection' like chocolate, baby!"

A QUIET BUT SIGNIFICANT shift in Emergence Christianity has been the rather marked increase, since 2009, in the number of national gatherings that bring together Emergences not only from all over the US, but also from offshore Emergence communities. Because of the expense of traveling to a venue, it has become the norm for those who are in physical attendance to twitter and Facebook and blog the work of the gathering in real time as it is happening. The result is that the audience for any such gathering is global and the impact immediate. When, as here, there is twittering in progress, both the twitter and the response as a rule are flashed on screens, allowing for a kind of running visible-to-all critique of the words being spoken. The result, in that case, is an appreciable enrichment of content and of the takeaway for everyone.

An Audience beyond the Audience

Control Room for Darkwood Brew

Emergence Christianity is as intimately tied to electronic and computer technology as Reformation Christianity was to the printing press. It is also just as dependent. The big difference is in how much less restricted and more fluid computer technology is than the press was and in how, as a result, it has enabled Emergence Christianity to be and continue to become what it is.

A precedent-breaking example of the new possibilities was effected in late 2010–early 2011 when, under the direction of Senior Pastor Eric Elnes, Countryside Community Church inaugurated Darkwood Brew in its Common Grounds Coffee House. In effect, Darkwood Brew is the world's first successful attempt to marry spiritual practice and transcendent worship with the machinations of interactive electronic delivery systems.

Last-Minute Prep with the Crew

That is, the technology shown in both these shots allows for the total integration in real time of the dozens and dozens of people gathered in Common Grounds with the hundreds in other congregations and worshipers gathered in both physicality and virtuality [cf. pp. P-18 and 19 on Koinonia]. Teachings can be done via Skype from all over the world, and questions engaged in personed exchanges. The result is something close to a potentially global worship and/or worshiping community. The apparent—but not real—paradox here is that, using all the cutting-edge technology available to it, Darkwood Brew is built primarily around the exploration, teaching, and exercise of ancient Christian spiritual practices, many of them, like *lectio divina*, Benedictine in origin.

Once a Shopping Mall, Now a Church

The term *mega-church* is a quantative rather than a qualitative descriptor, denoting worship communities in excess of two thousand congregants. Emergence Christianity, like every other presentation of the faith, has its fair share of mega's; and certainly among the best known, as well as most influential, of them is Mars Hill in Grandville, Michigan, a suburb of Grand Rapids.

True to Emergence sensibilities, rather than owning a traditional "church" space, the Mars Hill community is housed in—and uses every square inch of!—a once-defunct shopping mall. Worship services are held in what originally was the huge atrium of the mall and is now referred to affectionately as "The Shed."

A large part of every service in most Emergence worship is the "teaching." Shown here offering a teaching is Rob Bell, former senior teaching and founding pastor. Prominent in Emergence thinking and praxis, Bell has been one of the first leaders to understand the importance of sending the Emergence message out through commercial channels; and his *Nooma* videos have had an inestimable impact on Emergence praxis and spirituality in the US, Canada, the UK, and Europe.

Listening to a Sunday Morning Teaching at Mars Hill

Conferencing with Darkwood Brew at Koinonia

In the early days of this century, religion demographers were estimating that by the year 2010 as many as twenty million Americans would be having their entire worship and religious experience in cyberspace. That estimate seems now to have been as accurate as it was prophetic, and cyber church is a substantial part of Emergence Christianity.

Shown here are but two of many possible examples of cyber church and are taken from the virtual world of Second Life. The first is Koinonia, a Congregational church, and the second is 1st Presbyterian of Second Life (1PCSL). While each bears the name of a denominational tradition that is well known in physicality, neither is tightly affiliated with the institutional church whose name its own suggests. Both were, in fact, established by seminarians, not church officials.

Koinonia Congregational Church on Second Life

Prayer Group in Chapel of 1PCSL

1st Presbyterian Church of Second Life and Conference Center

Ecumenical Dinner on Second Life

The elaborateness of the campuses speaks for itself in both instances. In the same way, the small group arrangement of avatars in the Prayer Chapel of 1PCSL and in the Conference Room at Koinonia are not unlike small group formations in physicality. What may not be so apparent is that the Koinonia small group is in conference with Eric Elnes (cf. pp. P-14–15—Darkwood Brew) in real time. The Koinonia Community is also believed to have been the first virtuality communion to hold simultaneous and co-led worship between a congregation in physicality and one in virtuality, a feat it accomplished in 2009.

Ecumenism is a *desiratum* for Emergence in whichever world it may be. Seen here is a dinner meeting/planning session between some leaders of the 1PCSL and the Koinonia communities.

The Old as well as the Young

One of the more persistent, and perhaps most insidious, myths about Emergence Christianity is the notion that it is a phenomenon of the young. There are no data to define exactly the proportional numbers of Emergence Christians who no longer fall within the "Young" category; but experientially a careful observer would estimate that somewhere between a fourth and a third of Emergences in the US are in the older demographic. This shot, taken at Church in the Cliff in the Oak Cliff suburb of Dallas, Texas, is a poignant and gentle example of those proportions and of the interaction between young and old in worship.

For the first time in almost seventeen hundred years, Western Christians are having to face again the question of the relationship between church and state within the restrictions of faithful living. As religious practice and belief become more and more severed from political policy and practice, how to render unto Caesar what is Caesar's and unto God what is God's is an evolving and ever more intricate dance and is frequently referred to as the problem of "dual citizenship."

Communion Table—Fort Tryon Park, NY, May 2008

For Emergence Christians, the tension posits an especially difficult question and often seems to be one not of dual but of triple citizenship. That is, the integration required is that of living faithfully with the church, the state, and also the culture. The communion table shown here expresses symbolically and compellingly that delicate balance as flag and elements are joined as well by the double entendre of a chessboard and pieces. The use of the most complex game in our culture suggests not only the culture itself but also the tense carefulness and concentration required of those who would play successfully through to the end.

Street Party at The Simple Way Community in Philadelphia

Neo-monasticism is one of the more visible, and certainly one of the most rapidly expanding, segments of Emergence Christianity. That does not mean it is an easy way of life or one to be assumed lightly. Like any other form of monastic living, though, it can be a thing of joy that gives joy. The shot here is of a cooling-off street party in front of The Simple Way in Philadelphia. Most American Neo-monastic communities live and work in inner-city areas like the one shown here.

The "chef" flipping the burgers at the party is Shane Claiborne, one of the founders of The Simple Way community. He and Jonathan Wilson-Hartgrove are two of the principal leaders both in the US and beyond it of the Neo-monastic movement. Claiborne in particular has been a guiding force behind the establishment and growth of the Community of Communities, an international network that seeks to make it possible for Emergence communities to be in effective and effectual contact with one another.

Shane Claiborne Manning the Grill at The Simple Way

Courtesy of Franklin Golden

Jonathan Wilson-Hartgrove and *Common Prayer*

Jonathan Wilson-Hartgrove, cofounder with his wife, of Rutba House in North Carolina, is caught here by the camera just shortly after he has received from the publisher the first copies of *Common Prayer: A Liturgy for Ordinary Radicals* in December 2010. Spearheaded by Wilson-Hartgrove and done with Claiborne and Enuma Okoro, the book is as radical as its title suggests. More to the point, its publication marks a singular moment for Neo-monasticism which now has a breviary or prayer book suitable for all Emergence Christians and more or less essential for Neo-monastic ones.

Painting the Message in Philadelphia

WHILE MOST DENOMINATIONS and traditions within North American Christendom would regard themselves as "committed to missions," the term *missional*, when used by Emergence Christians, reaches far beyond an intellectual or theological commitment. It assumes, instead, a place and a way of being in the right-here and the right-now. For Emergences, missional happens in the neighborhood and the immediate. It is also beautiful and always gifting to all around it, while remaining true to its faith and its beliefs.

This painting, on the side wall of a house adjacent to an empty lot on "a pretty tough corner" in Philadelphia, is what Shane Claiborne of The Simple Way calls "very Trinitarian." It is also a quintessential example of missional in Emergence.

No segment of the ordained clergy is more affected by Emergence Christianity than are bi-vocational pastors and members of the permanent diaconate. Sometimes called tentmakers or self-supporting clergy, these men and women do not desire full-time congregational work, having chosen instead to work in the world as both ordained persons and also members of the secular workforce. Because Emergence communities are frequently too small in number to afford or even desire full-time clergy, tentmakers and deacons are discovering that the call upon them is growing exponentially. In an attempt to address this substantial shift, the national associations of both the Presbyterian Church and the Episcopal Church gathered into working sessions like the one shown here to begin to discern how best to discover, serve, or even plant such communities.

Joint Meeting of Association of Presbyterian Tentmakers and National Association of Self-Supporting Anglican Ministers—Outside Chicago, November 2010

The conference, which opened with a plea from the Presiding Bishop of the Episcopal Church that its deliberations be shared as quickly as possible with the larger Church, was attended as well by two or three representatives of similar British and European associations. Even more telling was the presence of representatives of three US seminaries. As they themselves noted, the shift in clerical roles is of utmost importance to seminaries as they try to adapt their curricula and content emphases to accommodate Emergence.

United States Christians of all persuasions tend to think of Emergence as an American phenomenon when, in reality, Emergence came to North America long after it had already begun to be visible and operative in many other parts of the latinized Christian world. One of the ironies of this is that a principal spokesman, theologian, and teacher within international Emergence is himself a Yankee, Brian McLaren.

McLaren, who is sometimes referred to as the Martin Luther of Emergence, spends much of his time in meetings and gatherings outside of the US, especially in Europe and much of Africa, where Emergence is known as *amahoro*. Here he is shown in a May 2010 consultation in Mombasa with amahoro leaders there.

Like the US, Canada has come more recently than have Europe, South America, Africa, and some parts of Asia to Emergence. One of the more invigorating results of that mutual tardiness has been a lively and growing exchange of ideas and camaraderie amongst Emergence Christians on both sides of the border. McLaren is shown here addressing just such an Emergence gathering in Victoria, British Columbia, also in 2010.

Right: Christ Church Cathedral, Victoria, BC

Below: Gathering Room, Mombasa, Kenya

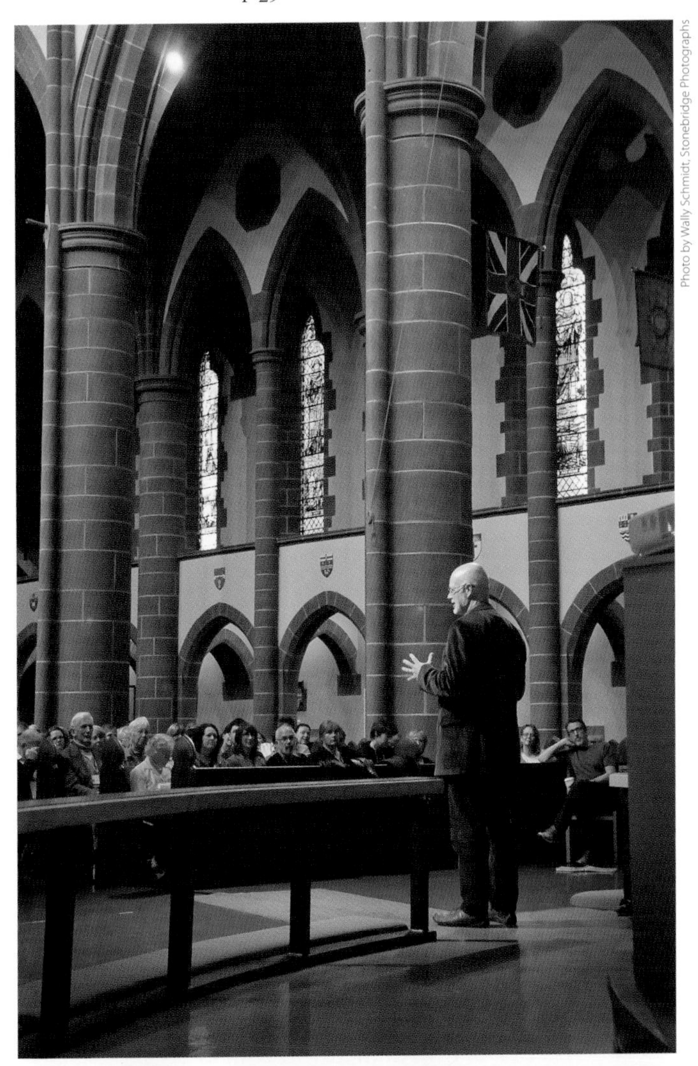

Photo by Wally Schmidt, Stonebridge Photographs

© 2011 Jaimi Kercher. Courtesy of Jaimi Kercher Photography.

SLOT Festival 2009. Each year many of those attending the SLOT Festival put up tent cities like this one. The festival is held each summer at an abandoned Cisterian Monastery near Lubiaz, Poland.

Music has always played a somewhat disproportionate role in matters of religious change and times of communion shifts. Certainly, its role in the shaping, broadcasting, and cohering of Emergence Christianity has proved to be so. Some would even argue that it has been unprecedented. Either way, the newer music and the festivals built around it have become principal vehicles for both spreading and celebrating the Word.

Probably the most famous of the Emergence festivals in Europe is the SLOT Arts Festival held annually in Poland. Tent cities, like the one shown here at SLOT 2009, are a hallmark of the festivals everywhere. They are also a major draw for many attendees. A week of music and theology and worship along with a week of camping out among friends and colleagues is an attractive concept for Emergences.

Courtesy of Becky Garrison

Communion at Greenbelt 2009. The festival is held each summer at Cheltenham Racetrack outside of London.

Within English-speaking Emergence, the grand dame of the festivals is Greenbelt, which attracts upward of twenty thousand participants every year. During a grueling week of worship, celebration, and conversation, some of the discussion allows as well for the exercise of ecumenical and ecclesial politics. While successful annual US festivals like Cornerstone in Illinois have themselves attracted twenty-plus thousand participants, some Emergence leaders had felt the need for a "more Greenbelt-like" festival. Accordingly, in June 2011, the Wild Goose Festival was inaugurated at Shakiri Hills in North Carolina. Time will tell whether or not Wild Goose can achieve the more international goals its conveners have set for it.

Emergence theology, as it has evolved—and is evolving—has evidenced an excitement and sophistication that are contagious as well as innovative and groundbreaking. The great theological minds of the mid-to-late twentieth century have proved themselves to be fertile background for further exploration and sometimes belated application. Bonhoeffer (martyred in 1945) in radical discipleship, Newbigin (1909–1945) in missiology, Karl Rahner (1904–1984) in shaping the new Catholicism of Vatican II, even Miroslav Volf (b. 1956) have all had their influence on Emergence thinking. But none has been more influential than Jürgen Moltmann (b. 1926) whose teachings about the Trinity, about the kingdom of God here as well as hereafter, about Christian hope in an abrasive relationship with secular society, etc., etc., have proved central to Emergence theology.

Reading Moltmann

Panning here for the camera behind an anthology of Moltmann's work and in lighthearted Emergence fashion is Tony Jones, himself a major seminal theologian and formative leader in Emergence theory and practice.

16

Post, Quasi, Whatever

Getting beyond the Vague

For a brief period in the not-too-distant past, it was fashionable for us to describe both our times and their newest expression of latinized Christianity as being "post" something or other. Thus, as a culture, we often described ourselves as being post-literate, post-Enlightenment, post-rational, etc. Vaguest of them all, of course, was post-modern. As a term, we rendered it fairly useless early on by our collective tendency to use it as a dumping bin for all those incongruities and disparate shifts we could not quite bring ourselves to analyze.

We also used some quasi-religious descriptors like post-Christendom, post-Protestant, and even occasionally post-denominational to describe our secular as well as our religious circumstances. Then there were some *post* terms like post-evangelical or post-sectarian that occurred almost exclusively in Christian, rather than secular, conversation. By any tallying, though, all of these "posts" and another half dozen or so like them are description by subtraction rather than by addition. Despite the fact that they are all true, they still are more negative than they are positive. So in restiveness, Emergence Christianity, along with Emergence in general, began to employ the positives, and the result is a rather breathtaking lexicon.

Deinstitutionalism and Hierarchy

Emergence Christianity is, first and foremost, deinstitutionalized, a fact we have already seen in our overview of its most apparent physical presentations. Deinstitutionalization is likewise a prime characteristic that Emergence Christianity shares completely and unequivocally with the culture at large. Many well-meaning, non-Emergence Christians find it almost obligatory to deplore the falling numbers in nationally established denominations and the shrinking congregations in local churches and parishes. Yet one has only to look at the declining membership statistics of, for example, the local Rotary Club, the Kiwanis International, the VFW, the American Legion, etc., to understand that deinstitutionalization is in no way restricted to churches and religious institutions. Rather, deinstitutionalization is a new value in our new times as well as a defining hallmark of Emergence Theory itself.

It has followed logically that where there was no interest in, or at best only passing regard for, institutions as such, a concomitant disaffection for hierarchy would surely follow.[1] The business of institutions almost always requires hierarchy, even as hierarchy by its very nature almost always works to surround itself with the safety and cushion of an institution. In essence, the two are inextricably entwined, one with the other. Since the older standing traditions of Christianity—Orthodoxy, Roman Catholicism, Anglicanism, and Protestantism—all function by hierarchy and presume its absolute necessity in their existence, there is a continuing disconnect between Emergence Christian sensibilities and all those other inherited ecclesial patterns and habits that function and run themselves by hierarchal means. Perhaps of all the disparities between the two, this one is the least amenable to adjudication and the most interruptive of ecumenical conversation. At least, it has proved to be so far.

Science, Paradox, and Politics

Both Emergence citizens in general and also Emergence Christians, wherever they live and within whatever context, are characterized by a few other qualities that can be almost as disruptive, at least in some situations and conversations. The first and perhaps the foremost among these is more age- or generationally tied than are some other of these telling characteristics. That is, those Emergences born since 1980 or thereabouts are far more comfortable with the physical sciences than are those born and reared prior to that time. This disconnect holds true, as a rule, even for older citizens who are themselves Emergence Christians.

Physics, in particular, has become the poetry underlying much Emergence theology, whether it is named as such or not. The comprehension of the universe and of creation and life rests upon principles, facts, and applications that, for younger Emergences, give a grandeur to faith and an excitement to theological conversation that are lost on most older Christians, whether they be in inherited church or in fresh expressions church. This disjuncture, caused by what is essentially an intellectual inequity, has proved to be an impediment of monumental proportions to the ability of established or institutional church leaders and fresh expressions church leaders to interface, especially in matters of belief.

Closely aligned with this almost unconscious integrating of science into belief and probably related to it at a psychological level is the Emergence penchant for paradox. And because they are comfortable with paradox, Emergence Christians are enormously comfortable with a both/and approach to life and faith. Where established church is accustomed to determining what may be allowed and what is to be accepted, Emergences are more open to considering whether or not two contending positions or contradictory assertions can be equally valid within context.

Secularly, we see this latter phenomenon of both/and in the gradual decline in political discussion of oppositional terms like "liberal" and "conservative" and also, though less obviously, of ones like "progressive." Religiously, we see it most dramatically in the movement away from (almost the aggressive rejection of) doctrinalism, dogmatism, and printed or sworn-to and "official" Statements of Faith or Belief. As terms, those words all name or imply a divide that can simply not be imagined, much less engaged, within an Emergence world of contextualized interpretation, shifting loyalties, and dialogical, both/and thinking.

Technology

Emergence Christianity also shares with the larger culture another major, informing, and sometimes ecclesially disjunctive characteristic. It is techno-savvy. In fact, it is highly unlikely that deinstitutionalizaton and nonhierarchical organization could even exist in either the secular or the religion realm were it not for techno-savvy and the internet. If the Reformation of five hundred years ago were facilitated and empowered by the printing press, as indeed was the case, then even that lurch forward pales in the face of what the computer and the Net have done for, to, and with the Great Emergence and all the pieces and parts thereof.

Because of those exact same factors of exponentially accelerated growth in information and in the surfeit of human conversation now available to us, and because of our immediate access to both of them, another, even more portentous, shift has happened. Thanks to electronics, we who live within the Great Emergence now enjoy a kind of heady connectedness to everything. But thanks to urban mobility in our jobs and to our constant reshuffling of the places where we live (both those things being unavoidable circumstances in the Great Emergence, of course), we increasingly feel unconnected to anything in particular. And as with our longing for ancient liturgy and earlier ways of being church, so too here in our secular lives. In our sense of rupture and dislocation, we ache for those simpler, more anchoring ways of human belonging that once were. Like it or not—and many critics of our times do not—we increasingly long for some "tribe" or coterie that will be both stable and transportable, a connection that, in order to go with us wherever we are, is nongeographic, nonpolitical, nonfamilial, and/or nonreligious in its cohesion.

We—all of us, whether we be religious or not—are neo-tribal to some greater or lesser extent. What that rather clunky expression seeks to name is a tendency or condition of considerable importance to Great Emergence cultures and social patterns in general. It is of especial importance for Christians living within the Great Emergence.

Dual and Triple Citizenship

Our Lord spoke of Caesar's kingdom and God's kingdom. It was a dichotomy that was comfortable to His hearers and that remained comfortable for some three hundred years thereafter. Render unto Caesar what is Caesar's and unto God what is God's made perfect sense. As a dual citizenship, it covered all the bases as well.

With the coming of the religio-political changes effected by Constantine in the fourth century, though, the two discrete entities of church and state came to be less and less discrete. Within a few decades, the church became bedfellow to the state, and the state became the agency that established the church. Allegiance to one was allegiance to the other, and disloyalty to one was immediate offense to the other. Christendom had been born, and for the next seventeen centuries, it would hold sway over latinized Christian culture, especially in Europe and, ultimately, in North America.

One of the constantly rumbling, endlessly grinding shifts of the peri-Emergence was the diminishment and, finally, the death of Christendom. By the turn of the last century, the rending of church and state back into their original configuration as separate and not always compatible entities was well on its way to completion. Likewise, by the turn of the century, the shift had already come to be an abrasive fact of life for those Christians whose religious beliefs conflict with what is required of them by the state.[2]

At an objective, less individualized level, though, what was really happening was the return to latinized life of dual citizenship and, inevitably for some, of divided loyalties. Unto Caesar what is Caesar's and unto God what is God's was back. But at the same time, and definitely behind the scenes and absent from the evening's headline news, a kind of third citizenship was also being born.

This new thing—this new center of loyalty and belonging and almost-tribal identity without historical precedent—was indeed a nongeographic, nonpolitical "culture" (for lack of a better word and because "culture" is less visceral than "tribal"). And that culture, however inadequately labeled, is an electronically enhanced and electronically facilitated place-of-being that is neither familial nor territorial nor inherently religious in its composition. We are who we hook up with wherever and whoever they are, and that is enough. Indeed, it is more than enough. It is prime and, by extension, primal.

Emergence Christians, who are deeply relational by predisposition, are acutely aware of this triple citizenship and of its implications.[3] They are most especially aware of it in their missional lives. There is another and third realm now, one among whose natives the faith must come to find its place, but what is spoken must be in the natives' own language, and what is done must not violate the integrity or stability of a native's loyalties—which is easier than it sounds for most Emergence Christians because most of them are themselves triple-citizenship natives.[4]

Emergence citizens do not live exclusively in this third and new situation, of course. They live, as we always have, in the physical world as well. Yet even here, the perception of an advancing interconnectedness of all things and all people has led, in both Emergence in general and in Emergence Christianity in particular, to a strong emphasis on social justice and on ecological concerns. Perhaps these two shared values, more than any other of the characteristics and principles held in common by the two bodies, are also, ironically enough, two of the most informing disconnects between them.

Social justice, as any good Great Emergence citizen will say, is just plain common sense in this time of glocalized connectedness, to use another new and awkward term. As a political stance, social justice is, in fact, little more than enlightened self-interest. Even the most persuaded atheist will routinely choose to serve in a soup kitchen or raise a house for the indigent or campaign for better and more equitable health care coverage. It makes no sense at all, fiscally let alone morally, for a society or group to not provide for the basic needs of all its members. If for no other reason, there is always the hard fact that the cost of repairing the results of such inequities usually far exceeds what the cost of prevention would have been.

To stand, then, behind political and charitable actions designed to alleviate the problems of the poor and disadvantaged, to spend time and money building shelter for those who have none, to go even to a distressed part of the world like Haiti, is to be sensible. As we have noted earlier, such is not, just by default, a Christian act. For, says Emergence Christianity, so long as "we" did this good and beneficial thing for "them," we have failed to act in the name and manner of Christ. The crevasse or abyss patent in the language of "our" doing this for "them" is immediate proof of that fact.[5]

It is, rather, only when we together, as progeny of God together, act in sacred affection to satisfy the unmet needs of some of the rest of us that we build or provide as Christians. As more than one Emergence Christian has been known to remark, "When I help build a house for somebody, I want it to be a home where I and my family would be welcome and where the new owners will be welcome in my house. When I help to provide food, I want it to be food shared among us easily and frequently. I'm not out to save the world, just to be part of it."

That distinction is not just a bit of rhetorical fancy or holy posturing. It is why one will find heavy concentrations of Emergence Christian gatherings in distressed urban neighborhoods and urban ghettos. It is why one could probably not find even two dozen Emergence Christians in most of the gated communities in this country. ("Jesus didn't live in a gated community, and He doesn't much want us to either," is the usual rebuff on this one.) It is why Emergence Christians think of themselves as communal and relational more than sacred or holy. It is also, inevitably, why most Emergence Christian communities or nodes or pods or cohorts or gatherings are unself-consciously diverse in every way, be it race, sexual preference, gender, socioeconomic class, or intellectual privilege.

In an analogous way, Emergence Christianity also shares with Great Emergence culture, as it is evolving and expanding among us, a strong dedication to greenness. But here again, as with social justice, there is a sharp distinction made by Emergence Christians between two operative sets of motivation. Like social justice, greenness can operate simply out of enlightened self-interest and something very akin to plain old horse sense, to use that rather graphic colloquialism. For the Emergence Christian, the horse sense and enlightened self-interest of secular greenness are no more Christian (nor un-Christian, for that matter) than are the horse sense and enlightened self-interest that appertain to secular participation in social justice. Greenness, for the Emergence Christian, is inextricably tied instead to a sense of divine direction or vocation. Emergence Christians operate unceasingly under the premise that this is God's creation we are living on, that it is our duty as well as our joy to care for rather than consume it, and that the Father's will is ever and always to be done as faithfully here as it is done in heaven.[6]

Of the several general characteristics that the Great Emergence and Emergence Christianity hold in common, these of deinstitutionalization; nonhierarchal organization; a comfortable and informed interface with physical science; dialogical and contextual habits of thought; almost universal technological savvy; triple citizenship with its triple loyalties and obligations; a deeply embedded commitment to social justice with an accompanying, though largely unpremeditated, assumption of all forms of human diversity as the norm; and a vocation toward greenness—these undoubtedly are among the most characterizing. They certainly are the ones we need to hold in mind as we turn our attention to considering the theological and architectural substructures of the thing we now recognize as Emergence Christianity.

NOTES

1. Silicon Valley is the quintessential example of this principle. Obviously dependent upon the computer, the Net, and techno-savvy at exquisite levels, it is also the best example available of the power of minimal hierarchy in corporate organization.

2. One thinks immediately, for example, of right-to-life physicians practicing in places where a woman's right to abortion is legally guaranteed. One must think as well of those who seek the presence of Scripture in public places or the use of God's name in the oaths spoken by those assuming public office. The list goes on, growing incident by incident on a daily basis in some part or other of old Christendom.

3. An excellent overview of the implications of relationality in Emergence society from the perspective of religion can be found in David Galston, "Postmodernism, the Historical Jesus, and the Church," in *The Fourth R*, September–October 2005, 11–15.

4. *Neo-tribalism*, as an area of study within contemporary sociology, means both far more and far less than one might assume from its brief employment here.

Likewise, there is a body of thought within Christianity itself that has contended for some time that the "third citizenship" should simply be given back its ancient label of *citizen of the world*. The connotations and implications of that expression militate, at least for many Christian leaders, against its formal use. There is, however, an emerging possible clarification and variant of that idea called *cosmopolitanism*. As a label, cosmopolitanism would seek to recognize both the third-citizenship phenomenon and also the missional, political, and social implications of such inevitable citizenship for Christians.

In this regard, as in so many other things in my life, I am indebted to Brian McLaren, who generously called to my attention the work of Namsoon Kang. Specifically, her chapter, "Toward a Cosmopolitan Theology: Constructing Public Theology from the Future," in *Planetary Loves: Spivak, Postcoloniality, and Theology* (ed. Stephen D. Moore and Mayra Rivera [Fordham University Press, 2011]), elegantly and eloquently presents these ideas. Anyone interested, even casually, in the implications of third citizenship would do well to engage with Kang on those pages.

Interested readers may also want to look at the work of Bruce Bimber, professor emeritus in political science and information theory at University of California, Santa Barbara. The term *accelerated pluralism* comes out of Bimber's extensive and highly respected study of this new phenomenon of a third citizenship or of the elimination of the "village" for identity and the insertion instead of urban cliques.

5. Emergence Christians will sometimes refer to such as being "acts of inhumane kindness." As expressions go, that one is certainly tart as well as clarifying.

6. *Saving Paradise: How Christianity Traded Love of This World for Crucifixion and Empire* (Beacon, 2008) by Rita Nakashima Brock and Rebecca Ann Parker addresses the subject and religious implications of greenness with great clarity, objectivity, and thoroughness. It should be required reading for all contemporary Christians, be they Emergences or not.

17

The Whole and Its Parts

Bringing It All Together

> Probably the largest reformation of all times in Church history is in full swing. It is the combination of a threefold current initiative of God: moving from church to Kingdom as our legal base; moving from pastoral, teacher-based and evangelistic to apostolic and prophetic foundations; and departing from a market-based behavior to a kingdom-shaped economy.[1]

Wolfgang Simson, an Emergence Christian leader and theolog in Germany, wrote those words in November 2009, when Emergence Christians were struggling to regain their balance and self-understanding. As a summary of what Emergence Christianity is and toward what it is moving, however, Simson's declaration still stands today as one of the most succinct and elegant of them all.[2]

What Simson describes is the context and impetus out of which Emergence Christianity, as a construct, comes, and that toward which it moves; and as such is an entirely legitimate and defensible position from which to speak. Emergence Christianity is a whole. Like most wholes, however, it is composed of member parts, and those parts are where we want next to go.

Protestantism was born five hundred years ago as a construct, a whole, a conversation, a way of looking at the world. To this very day, most of us can list quite readily those same major ideas and values that still characterize Protestantism, that still define it, that still make it instantly recognizable to us wherever we meet it. Yet acknowledging that those things are true in no way belies the fact that Protestantism, for all its recognizable and distinctive characteristics, is not a whole. Rather it is a construct of parts, and those parts differ from one another every bit as sharply as Protestants differ from Roman Catholics or both of them from Eastern Orthodox Christians. Nor did anyone ever, ever, ever think that Lutherans, for example, are the same as Baptists or that Mennonites should be regarded as identical to Presbyterians. No, Protestantism is a distinct and shared ethos with differing and distinct member parts.

As with Protestant Christianity, so with Emergence Christianity: a distinct and shared ethos with differing and distinct member parts. And as with Protestantism, so with Emergence in one other way: the earliest Protestants were deeply inclined toward seeing themselves as one body, a kind of whole against the opposing forces of the Christendom in which they lived. There were differences in theology and praxis, even before the Ninety-Five Theses were tacked on Wittenberg's church door, but those were kept in abeyance, insofar as possible. It was not until 1529 that those varieties of opinion could no longer be contained. In October of that pivotal year, Martin Luther and Huldrych Zwingli, along with eight other Reform leaders, met at Marburg Palace to try to reconcile the discrepancies and disjunctures in their understanding of the faith and its proper practice, but such was not to be. While they could agree on many things—on most things, in fact—they could not agree on the nature of the Eucharist. Were the bread and wine the actual body and blood of the Christ? Luther said yes, Zwingli said no. Or were they representations of the body and blood? Zwingli said yes, Luther said no. Protestant denominationalism was off and running.

And if that statement seems cynical, it is not so intended. Rather, as part of maturation for any body, be it a child's growing one or a construct of learned and godly men in congress, a construct must discover its unity by discovering its parts. Without that requisite step, there is no maturity, nor is there any ability to employ the parts to the benefit and sustenance of the whole. Emergence Christianity has its member parts and, in 2010, it had its Marburg.

Emergence/Emerging/Emergent

At a popular level, the two best-known or most often referenced groups within Emergence Christianity are Emerging Church and Emergent Church or, if one prefers, Emerging Christianity and Emergent Christianity. During the first three or four years after the creation of Emergent Village, the two terms of *emerging* and *emergent* were still being used interchangeably, even by leaders like McLaren and theologians like D. A. Carson. As interchangeable terms, they denoted not only the two groups but also the whole construct of Emergence Christianity itself in all of its presentations.

That kind of conflation still occurs sometimes in general conversation, though with decreasing frequency. A growing sophistication about what actually is and is transpiring has led both the general public and Emergence Christians themselves to employ more precise, and therefore, more useful labels. Both Emerging Christianity and Emergent Christianity are presentations of Emergence Christianity, but neither of them is the whole sum of it, nor is either of them to be confused with the other.

Emergent Church or Christianity or Christians are those associated, especially in this country and the United Kingdom, with Emergent

Village. They are the leaders, thinkers, theologs, and everyday Christians who see that loose, web-based confederation as their home base and who regard everyone who composes it as colleagues and confreres in the kingdom. Arguably, in the 1980s or even in the 1990s, those same men and women, had they had occasion to do so, would have probably referred to themselves as also "emerging," for the coming of Emergent Village was, in essence, no more than a forking within the branches of the Emergence tree. There are now, however, distinct differences between the two.

The differences between Emerging and Emergent are, as one would expect, both theological and practical. Emergent Christianity/Village/Church/Christians are aggressively all-inclusive and nonpatriarchal. They are far more interested in the actuality of Scripture than in its historicity or literal inerrancy. Holding that there is an incredible human arrogance involved in thinking that we can—or should—reduce God to the outlines and bullet points of our logic, they decry such conversations, seeking instead to find the Spirit being revealed rather than some kind of arbitrary uniformity within the contextualized specifics. By and large, Emerging Christianity/Church/Christians could not differ with these positions more strongly if they tried.

Interestingly enough, Emerging Christians are nearer to Hyphenateds than one might at first realize. Like Hyphenateds, they want to infuse Emergence methods and proclivities into worship, but they wish also to retain traditional theology. Unlike Hyphenateds, however, they do not come with a shared, inherited liturgy or praxis nor with any kind of uniform creedal corpus. As a result, Emerging is usually patriarchal in its worship style and understanding of right order. It condemns homosexuality as biblically forbidden, though it increasingly tends to accept homosexuals into fellowship; and it tends to emphasize the experience of worship itself, the spiritual practice of "church," and the shape of it as welding together a kingdomlike body of believers. Despite their differences, however, they both are Emergence, for both evidence the hallmarks of the Great Emergence and the culture that has resulted from its coming.

Ten Questions

Emergence Christianity's Marburg, when it happened in 2010, was in many ways the point at which Emerging and Emergent finally had to agree to disagree. In that year, Brian McLaren released a book, *A New Kind of Christianity: Ten Questions That Are Transforming the Faith.*[3] If *A Generous Orthodoxy* had been, as it was, the Emergence analog to Luther's Ninety-Five Theses, then *A New Kind of Christianity* was most surely the Emergence analog to Luther's "Here I Stand" declaration of faith and principles in 1521.

McLaren's ten questions were but mother hen to a whole flock of lesser ones and dealt with everything from the place and proper use of Scripture to the location of authority and the question of Christian exclusivity in a multifaith universe. The howl of protest over his proposed answers was as loud almost as were the opposing cries of affirmation. Skilled theologians like Scot McKnight, who had always proclaimed himself as emerging/emergent, now went on record as Emerging, no longer Emergent. Pastors like Mark Driscoll of Mars Hill Church in Seattle, who had claimed and operated originally under the two labels as interchangeable, now reemphasized his place as Emerging and not Emergent in any way, shape, or form. Emerging Christianity and Emergent Christianity would forever be distinguishable one from the other, both between themselves and before the world at large.[4]

Neo-Monastics

After the Emerging and Emergent branches, probably the best-known or most frequently mentioned presentation of Emergence

Christianity per se is the Neo-monastics. In part, this is due to the fact that Neo-monastic practice itself is both counterintuitive for modernists and totally reasonable for citizens of the Great Emergence. In part, the visibility has to do with the fact that living in vowed community for the sake of the kingdom makes good copy for reporters looking for the agreeably unusual or just faintly outré. In part, it certainly has to do with the fact that Neo-monasticism was one of the earliest expressions of Emergence Christianity in the latinized Christian world and, therefore, has had time to mature. And in part, it has to do with the fact that, like Emergent Christianity, Emergence Neo-monasticism enjoys a loose confederation known as the Community of Communities that grants some connectivity and cohesion to individual houses. But part—and, arguably, the real and most informing part—of Neo-monasticism's disproportionate presence in the public's awareness has to do with the fact that it has been Christianity from the beginning, or at the very least comes in unbroken, though shifting, lineage from the earliest days of the faith. It is also, again arguably, the most gospel-defined and/or governed of Christianity's corporate forms.

There are thousands of Neo-monastic communities in the latinized world, hundreds of them in this country. Sometimes they are small, no more than a handful of Christians living together to support one another in prayer and in doing the physical and spiritual work of the kingdom now and here. Sometimes they are large. Always, they are radical in their insistence on living with intentionality. Their practice can vary from simply sharing living quarters with common prayer and study time, to the practice of common table and common purse, to the practice of obedience and the pledge of stability, to even the outer limits of celibacy. As varied as their communities are, the impact of the Neo-monastics upon not only the physical world they occupy but also upon the thinking and praxis of other Emergence Christians is nonetheless inestimable. When the history of the first century or two of

Emergence Christianity is written, theirs will be one of the central themes or divisions to be traced not only for itself but also for its formative presence within the larger body.

House Church

For sheer physical numbers (one must sometimes count heads, even in Emergence discussions), the largest coterie or division within Emergence Christianity is the house church. In this country alone, estimates of the number of people attending house church vary broadly in accord with the definition of "house church" being employed by the demographer. Every survey is content, however, to say that millions of Americans regularly attend, and have their whole worship and religious life in, a house church.[5] In aggregate, though, the house church segment within Emergence Christianity does not call itself by that name, at least not formally. It is Simple Church or sometimes Organic Church and, like Emergent and Neo-monasticism, enjoys a loose kind of confederacy in House2House.

There is also an intriguing distinction among many house churches. That is, some are composed primarily of natal Protestants, while others are composed primarily of natal Roman Catholics. There is no study to date of the numerical proportions between the two groups, but the Pew Forum did find in 2009 that 9 percent of natal Protestants in this country attended *only* house church.[6]

For natal Roman Catholics, there is another variation on the general theme. While their numbers, both as individuals and as coteries, are untallied, there is a separate—or at least specific—web-based affiliation, www.intentionaleucharisticcommunities.org. Additionally, many of the primarily or exclusively Roman house groups maintain a kirk-and-chicks format in which they have contact—and often very close affiliation—with a parish church or cathedral. It is in this segment of Emergence that some of the most earnest work is being done with regard to the role of the diaconate, the non-parish priest, and the mid-judicatories.

Missionals

One of the major characteristics of Emergence Christianity is its sense of being apostolic or, better put perhaps, of being called to the life of being called out in a radical way. That is, Emergence in general believes that, like the early apostles, Christians are called out in order to be sent back in. We are here as apostles in the fullest and most historic sense of that vocation. Brian McLaren, with his customary way, has pinpointed with great accuracy the problem, not with this attitude, but with trying to name and describe it:

> This idea of sent-in-ness is far more radical than most of us realize. . . . The word people are using to capture this idea—that we are called-out-so-we-can-be-sent-back-in—is *missional*. Sadly, it's already become a kind of buzzword in many settings, meaning little more than "really serious about evangelism" or "intentional" or "cool and hip."[7]

McLaren wrote those words in 2009, and the semantic diffuseness he bemoans has only grown worse, not better, in the intervening years. Is "missional" a conversation within Emergence? A movement? An informing attitude? Or is it rather an entity, a member-part?

Probably the answer to all those questions is yes. But the fact that those attitudes and conversational themes pervade all of Emergence does not, in the final analysis, preclude the presence of a unit or component part within Emergence that is distinctly focused on that characteristic or emphasis.

The result for Missionals of the confusion in identity has been to give their particular exercise of Emergence a kind of cachet. It has also caused them, inadvertently, to move through a documentable evolution of sorts. The consequence of all that is that they are perhaps the most absorbing and easiest subset in Emergence to study. Few branches or limbs within Emergence have generated the kind of scholarly study that Missional has. *The Missional Church in Perspective: Mapping Trends and Shaping the Conversation* stands as one of the most careful and elucidating studies to date of any single part within Emergence Christianity.[8]

Likewise, a convoluted genesis has led to the creation of what has to be one of the most colorful and jauntiest, as well as the most deadly serious, networks in all of Emergence. transFORM is, to quote its own words, "a missional community formation network."[9] It is, more to the point, a network of networks, a coming together into one conversational opportunity, of all the various permutations of Missional that are functioning and willing, be they simply a theme within an established church congregation or a bunch of over-the-top Emergence clergy calling themselves the Outlaw Preachers.[10]

Whatever the various presentations involved and whatever that spectrum may be, transFORM is pure Missional Emergence. That purity rests in its thrust toward the formation and sustaining of communities of practice that in every way are evidences of God's kingdom on earth as well as active agents within it and proclaimers of it by word and action. What it shall become is yet to be determined, perhaps, but what it has come from is more various than any other grouping in Emergence, and that, in and of itself, would suggest a various and possibly even dramatic future.

Hyphenateds

Along with the Missionals, the Hyphenateds are the only other group within Emergence Christianity to have been, to date, the subject of a book-length treatment. That fact should not surprise one, however; for like the Missionals, the Hyphenateds are not only very colorful, but they are also as divergent and various as are the traditions they come from and refuse to totally leave. *The Hyphenateds: How Emergence Christianity Is Re-Traditioning Mainline Practices* is a compendium of fourteen essays by practicing Hyphenated clergy.[11] The essays, in their titles as in their content, run the gamut. As titles, ones like "Why Luthermergent? Because we always have been and better be now and forevermore, or we aren't really Lutheran" by Nate Frambach or "Improvising with Tradition: A Case (Self) Study" by Timothy Snyder accurately convey not only the content of what is being said but also the playful, desperately serious tone with which it is being said. More important, however, those titles, like the volume's, speak to the singular position of the Hyphenateds within Emergence itself.

In many ways, Hyphenateds are not only Emergence Christians but are also the conduits between Emergence Christianity and inherited and/or institutional Christianity, a highway of sorts between Antioch and Jerusalem, a social media between what is coming and what has been. And this to the benefit of all.

There are problems with Emergence Christianity—limitations, vulnerabilities, susceptibilities—that will have to be worked out or worked around or maybe just accepted, as the case may turn out to be. That has always been true of whatever new form of the faith has arisen in one of our semi-millennial upheavals. But one of the problems that has beset previous emerging forms of the faith may not beset Emergence. That is, one of the dangers in pushing against what is and in striving toward a "purer" identity and praxis that are independent of it lies in the possibility of going too far.

The seductive pull of correcting what is seen as "the evil that has beset us" is quite capable of becoming the siren call that entices all the sailors over the edge and into the watery abyss of unembodied innovation waiting below. Hyphenateds, by their conversation, offer a cautionary tale about that danger, and by their presence, they offer a remedy. Take from the tradition, they say, what is spiritually meaningful and religiously formative and entwine it into what you are doing. Put more colloquially—which is the form of rhetoric most Hyphenateds use—the message is, "Don't throw out the baby with the bathwater."

But the Hyphenateds are conduits, and conduits, by definition, flow in two directions. While they may be carrying the ancient, the tried, and the exquisitely honed into Emergence thought, they are also infusing into their natal traditions the sensibilities, contextualized theology, and reinvigorated praxis of the Emergence Christian community that they likewise refuse to leave. It is, as a result, defensible to contend, as many observers now do, that it is the Hyphenateds who ultimately may prove to be the unique group. They move with no animosity toward either what has been or what is becoming. The result is an impunity that grants them effectual credence in both camps. Nothing could be more singular than that, or more laden with possibilities.

All of which brings us to a bit of a conundrum, though hardly an earth-shattering one. That is, the question of whether or not Fresh Expressions is a form of Hyphenated Emergence, or is instead a freestanding, distinctly definable entity rising out of the Hyphenated experience. The phrase "fresh expression(s) of church," as we have seen, originated in 2004 with the Church of England's release of the report of its Mission and Public Affairs Council, *mission-shaped church*.

That report, in conjunction with the release that same year of McLaren's *A Generous Orthodoxy*, led the archbishop of Canterbury to establish the Office of Fresh Expressions as a deliberate attempt to enable and advance the new theology, missiology, liturgy, and ecclesiology that both *mission-shaped* and McLaren were talking about. Cosupported and coadministered by the Methodist Church in the United Kingdom and then joined later by other ecclesial bodies, Fresh Expressions became rather rapidly what it is today: an international network across denominational lines of presentations of Christianity that have been "established primarily for the benefit of people who are not yet members of any church" and that "have the potential to become a mature expression of church shaped by the gospel and the enduring marks of the church and for its cultural context."[12] Increasingly, that is, Fresh Expressions seems to be well on its way to becoming the first demonstrable gleanings of that colorful and various future predicted for the Hyphenateds.

In cataloging the variety of presentations which Emergence Christianity has assumed, it was customary for several years to list, in addition to those above, Alternative Worship or, as it is sometimes called, Alt Worship, as a distinct segment of the whole. While that phrase is still heard from time to time, it increasingly is employed nowadays in a somewhat adjusted way. That is, it generally now refers to those variations and adaptations within established congregations that have been created for the express purpose of appealing to and retaining their more restive congregants and neighbors. Kester Brewin once again crystallizes the situation when he says:

> Alternative worship groups are rarely conjunctive organizations, and it seems more likely to me from my inside view that alternative worship will be seen in the future to have been part of the preparation of the ground for the new to emerge from, rather than the newness itself.[13]

There are other small groups within Emergence, most of them too new and/or too small still (and/or some of them too self-indulgent, admittedly) for anyone, including themselves, to know what, if any, contribution they will eventually make to the overall configuration of Emergence Christianity a century or two hence. There are others—and Deep Church comes to mind here—that are conversations of great substance and that may find their role ultimately to be that of infusing with richness what is becoming, rather than of serving as bodies of practice themselves. Time will tell. But time will also tell us a great deal more than we presently know about what, in all of this, is the most uncharted and unavoidable ecclesial body within Emergence. That is, we must turn now to cyber church.

Cyber Church

The very word *cyber* connotes unmapped space. We move toward it as travelers eager to make the journey into whatever new thing or territory it proffers—either that, or we dig in our heels and scream out our refusals to go there ever again. Whichever camp any of us is in makes little difference. The fact is that technology has changed every single thing about our lives, including the fact that even locality itself has morphed into something very different from what it once was.

We human beings are locally where our bodies are, of course, and always have been. But . . . but we now are also locally where our computers or iPhones or PDAs have taken us, albeit noncorporeally. Both "places" exist in reality or, put another way, we "really" exist in and "really" experience both of them, according to where we are at any given time. Consequently, we now have two labels with which to name the two realms. We speak of physicality and of virtuality, recognizing both of them, when we do so, as extant and habitable realms.

As surely as we can and do conduct business in cyberspace, maintain our social and familial connections there, inform ourselves constantly about events impacting our lives there, and expand our information banks to accommodate to our changing needs for tricks and techniques as well as facts there, so too we can now worship in cyberspace. In point of fact, millions of us already do.[14]

Church in virtuality is to church in corporeality as banking in virtuality is to banking in corporeality. That is, the two are not at all the same, except . . .

. . . except, if we are honest, the banking does get done either way. The money moves around, the bills get paid, and the whole Net-based thing beats the heck out of using the drive-thru window with its always slightly greasy, pullout, sliding drawer . . . and it is the "except" that increasing numbers of Emergence pastors and parishioners acknowledge with a wry kind of smile and a slight nod of the head.

Unlike the other segments of Emergence Christianity that we have looked at, cyber church is not a unity held together by the intangibles of theological or practical persuasions. Rather, cyber church is a whole unto itself based on circumstances—on where it exists, not how. As a result, it can present in as many different postures and from as many differing belief-and-praxis stances as it wishes. It will still be cyber church so long as it is functioning within virtuality and not physicality. Presumably, in another hundred years or so, such a position and a lumping together of complexities will seem incredibly naïve or simplistic. For the time being, however, and for as long as we are caught within our own innocence about what can be, cyber church is Christian church in virtuality, and Christian church in virtuality, regardless of its postures and positions, is cyber church.

Presently, the most accessible—or perhaps, just the most informing—way for most of the simply curious to experience cyber church is through Second Life or through conversation with those who have worshiped there. Second Life is a virtual world that duplicates the physical world in all the overt, obvious ways, except that its citizens are avatars. That is, the "people" living in Second Life are pixel-made projections of people who physically are in physicality while being psychologically or subjectively in virtuality and engaging that experience through the avatar who is their presence while there. Clear? Perhaps not. Or perhaps just a bit mind-boggling. Either way, whether the mind is boggled or just simply amused by the boggling in others, cyber church cannot be ignored.

In Second Life there are, literally, innumerable churches, mosques, synagogues, and places of worship. Each has its own clergy or worship leaders, just as each has its own congregation or gathering of the faithful. Within most of the Christian gatherings, there is some greater or lesser contact between the cyber church in virtuality and the church, denomination, or group in physicality that is its analog and often its sponsor. Thus, the Anglican communion has a substantial cathedral on Epiphany Island in Second Life that has five clergy, all ordained, and that operates under the Episcopal oversight of the Bishop of Guilford in the United Kingdom. Likewise, purportedly the first joint worship ever to be held by cyber church and physical church together was conducted in September 2009 between a UCC congregation in Atlanta and the congregation of avatars gathered in the UCC-affiliated cyber church on the Isle of Koinonia in Second Life. And so it goes.

The most immediately relevant point for our purposes here, however, is that there is a vast new mission field in what we call virtuality and that it will, in all likelihood, be Emergence Christianity and Emergence Christians who are apostles to it. The next relevant point is that a veritable horde of questions arises the minute the physical faith enters the virtual world: Can an avatar priest consecrate pixel-based elements? Can he or she hear confession? Can he or she absolve? Can sacred unions be consecrated in virtuality? Can prayers be said there? Can we assume the presence in worship there of the Holy Spirit? Of God? Of Jesus? Et cetera.[15]

And now the mind—every mind—is boggled by the implications. Not only will those and other questions have to be answered, but two things must be said about the answering of them. First, the answering will largely be done by Emergence Christians in terms of an Emergence understanding of the faith; and second, whatever the answers are, they will wash back into physicality and influence or shape or modify the traditional or established answers within the physical church to those areas of thought and practice being questioned.

There is one other thing that must be said here. From the modernist point of view, one of the great roadblocks to accepting cyber church as valid is the lack of physical contact or human intimacy implicit in it. For many—perhaps the majority?—of especially the younger citizens of the Great Emergence, that lack is a virtue, not a deterrent, an attraction and not a detractor. Emergence Christians speak often about what is called either "anonymous intimacy" or "intimate anonymity." Either way, the phrase means to name that singular circumstance of Net-based life in which the removal of all threat of face-to-face contact opens the soul to expose itself to another with abandon and, thereby, to gain the relief of total openness. Such is, and will be, a major component of all thinking about cyber church and its role in Christianity over the coming centuries.

Not all cyber worship occurs exclusively in virtuality, of course. That would be far too easy. Rather, in the hands of some Emergence pastors, there is a form or site or blend—there is not yet a precise word that works—that binds experience in physicality and experience in virtuality together into one experience.

The practice of having a large church open up what is called "TV campuses" is hardly new. For years, a number of such bodies, most of them mega-churches, have set up satellite halls or meeting rooms for those who want to "go to church" but cannot, for one reason or another, "go" to the mother church literally. By going to the satellite site, the gathered join in hymns, announcements, and events specific to their satellite community while worshiping via television with the mother or hosting church during some of the liturgy and all of the sermon or teaching. This paradigm has been used primarily within evangelical circles. Now, however, rising out of the Emergence Christian ethos, there is a variation upon a theme—or, in truth, a whole new twist. Darkwood Brew, coming out of Countryside Community Church in Omaha, is the first and still prime example of this new approach.

Scott Griessel, writing for the UCC magazine *Still Speaking*, opened his 2011 coverage of Darkwood Brew by saying:

> Trying to describe Darkwood Brew is tough. Even those who produce and participate in the online services stumble when asked, "Well, what is it?"
>
> It's a web-based television show exploring emerging Christian faith. It's a wildly interactive technological focus point for thoughtful people. It's a top-notch jazz venue. It's an interview show. It's a resource for small groups. It's a 12th-century contemplative practice. It's renegade exploration at Christianity's outer edges. It's an espresso bar. It's communion. A lot of people love it.
>
> You might not like it.[16]

Griessel then takes five more pages to try to present the previously impossible in terms that are accessible to those still reacting only in terms of the traditionally possible.

Darkwood Brew itself is the pastoral child of Eric Elnes, long a leader in Emergence theology and also ecclesiology. As pastor of Countryside, Elnes has been able to divert some of Countryside's space, staff, resources, and Emergence fervor into creating a Sunday night service that is fully Emergence in ambience and includes an elegant coffee bar with baristas for those physically present, a top-notch jazz band, just as Griessel reports, and the immediate presence of fellow worshipers from all over the globe. The teaching is either Skyped in by an off-site guest speaker or, when Elnes is teaching, Skyped or Netcast out to all those who are participating off-site. The interaction with the speaker after the teaching—always an important part of most Emergence worship—is also done by Skype or via the Net. Contemplative devotion and liturgical worship are likewise simultaneous amongst those in Omaha and those in whatever corner of the earth they may be dwelling in. The result is a congregation of the faithful that is now operating within all three of the possible areas of human citizenship.

Welcome to Emergence Christianity, now available wherever you are, be it in this world or some other.

NOTES

1. For those who want to know more, Simson's 2009 book, *The Starfish Manifesto*, for which these words served as a public introduction, is available for download as a pdf file at www.starfishportal.net. The quotation itself may be seen in context at Simson's November 8, 2009, blog, under "The Starfish Manifesto Released," http://tallskinnykiwi.typepad.com/tallskinnykiwi/2009/11/.

2. A major document, *The Manifesto* was released in October 2009 at the Antioch Gathering, a convocation of some seventy-plus missional leaders from around the world meeting in Seleucia, a site chosen for its place in the apostolic and missional history of the early church.

3. San Francisco: HarperOne.

4. McKnight's eloquent and deeply considered critique of McLaren's "Here I Stand" position in *A New Kind of Christianity* was published in the March 2010 issue of *Christianity Today* (pp. 59–61ff.). It stands as a classic document in the evolution of contemporary Christianity and should command the attention of every Christian who is concerned with that process.

Likewise, Mark Driscoll, who had begun his separation from Emergent church in the mid and late nineties, stands as an outspoken voice in the growing tension between the two camps. Driscoll's effect and influence are hardly limited to the Mars Hill Church itself, however. He is the founder and guiding hand behind The Resurgence which, as its name suggests, was and is directed toward combining Great Emergence realities and sensibilities with an aggressive thrust toward more doctrinal and historically-evolved Christianity. The best-known physical presentations of Driscoll's and Resurgence's presence are probably the Acts 29 movement and network of churches and The Resurgence Training Center (Re:Train) which is dedicated to the advanced training of pastors in the principles and theology of the movement.

5. On August 31, 2009, the Barna Group released the first—and to date only—massive study of house church figures in the United States, entitled "Barna Update—08/31/2009—How Many People Really Attend a House Church? Barna Study Finds It Depends on the Definition." The opening paragraph précising the rather lengthy findings notes what it calls "significant" differences in data according to the definitions used. Those numbers, Barna reports, range "from a minimum of 4% of the adult population to a maximum of 33%!" The full Update may be found at http://www.barna.org/barna-update/article/19-organic-church/291-how-many-people-really-attend-a-house-church-barna-study-finds-it-depends-on-the-definition?q=organic+church or by contacting the Barna Group at tgorka@barna.org.

Readers who wish to know more about Simple Church may also want to read *The House Church Book: Rediscover the Dynamic, Organic, Relational, Viral Community Jesus Started* by Wolfgang Simson, with foreword by George Barna (Tyndale, 2009).

6. As taken from a release by the Associated Press on July 21, 2010, as reported by Linda Stewart Ball.

7. Brian McLaren, "One, Holy, Catholic and Fresh?" in *Ancient Faith, Future Mission: Fresh Expressions in the Sacramental Tradition*, ed. Steven Croft, Ian Mobsby, and Stephanie Spellers (New York: Seabury Books, 2010), 17.

8. Craig Van Gelder and Dwight J. Zscheile, *The Missional Church in Perspective: Mapping Trends and Shaping the Conversation* (Grand Rapids: Baker Academic, 2010).

9. *See* http://www.transformnetwork.org.

10. The "network of networks" is standard operating procedure for all the segments of Emergence and should not be seen as unique just to Missional Emergence. The point being made here is that transFORM and other sites like http://missionalchurchnetwork.com/shapevine-a-community-of-collaborators/ are robust and immediately obvious examples of what such forms of horizontal organization look like and how they can operate.

11. Phil Snydar, ed., *The Hyphenateds: How Emergence Christianity Is Re-Traditioning Mainline Practices* (St. Louis: Chalice Press, 2011).

12. As formally stated by the Fresh Expressions office and taken from their website, http://www.freshexpressions.org.uk/about/whatis. Accessed 24 June 2011.

13. Kester Brewin, *Signs of Emergence* (Grand Rapids: Baker, 2007), 93.

14. There are no current studies, so far as I have been able to discover, that give us the actual number of virtuality worshipers. As early as 2007, however, some demographers were predicting that by 2010 as many as twenty million Americans would be having their whole religious experience on the internet.

15. Because of its rather acute importance, there is a growing bibliography of vetted and sound material about cyber church. Of particular interest, Kimberly Knight's "Sacred Space in Cyberspace," in *Reflections* (Yale Divinity School, fall 2009), 43–46, is a practitioner's introduction to the whole construct. Knight is the founding pastor of the UCC Koinonia Community in Second Life.

There is now a Confession of Faith for the Church in Virtual Worlds that is the work of an aggregate of pastors ministering in virtuality and is available upon request from Neal Locke at neal@mrlocke.net. Locke himself is a founding member of 1st Pres in Second Life and the author of several significant papers on the subject.

At a more popular level, interested readers may wish to see Elizabeth Drescher's *Tweet If You ❤ Jesus: Practicing Church in the Digital Reformation* from Morehouse Publishing, discussed in the annotated bibliography.

16. "Stirring Things Up at Darkwood Brew," *Still Speaking*, spring–summer 2011, 46–51.

18

Finding the Big Story

The Role of Philosophy and Meta-Narrative

> Theology is shaped by the predilections of those who are doing it . . . or, at the very least, the approaches to it are shaped and contextualized by them. As a result of the pervasiveness of those subtle influences, all theological principles inevitably are shaped and contextualized.[1]

While that kind of statement seems perfectly obvious and reasonable to most of us who live as twenty-first-century Americans, it would have been neither obvious nor reasonable to our compatriots of the nineteenth, or even of the early twentieth, century. Theology, for those forebears of ours, would have been no more or less than systemized commentary and doctrinal elaboration upon the great meta-narratives of life. Or, more correctly put, perhaps, whatever theology one might have adhered to would have differed from the theology of another only in terms of whose interpretation of the various meta-narratives had been taken as a commonly held beginning point.

Of course, the great truth in all of this is that most people, were they God-fearing or not, would have spent their entire lives in the nineteenth and early twentieth centuries without ever once hearing the word *meta-narrative*, much less having to worry about the theological implications associated with it. No, popular concern with meta-narrative—which basically is a ten-dollar word for "the BIG story"—is singularly a function of Great Emergence thinking, and most specifically a direct result of peri-Emergence philosophy. It is, therefore and perhaps unfortunately, impossible to speak even cursorily about Emergence Christian theology without commencing with twentieth-century philosophy and meta-narrative.

Every age in Western history has had its great philosophers, and every age in Western history has had its popular or general thinking modified—albeit many decades after the fact, as a rule—by what those philosophers taught as the correct way to conceptualize the world and live in it. That having been said, it is entirely possible that history may look back on our time and find the impact of our peri-Emergence philosophers upon the contemporary lives and decisions of everyday citizens to be singular in its immediacy and its breadth.

Philosophy

Philosophy is, among other things, the meeting point between the sciences and the humanities. Arguably, much of the current immediacy and breadth of impact of twentieth-century philosophy has had, and still has, to do with the fact that, whatever else it may be, the Great Emergence is the age of science in every way, and any juncture between it and the rest of life has become a hope-filled and desirable place to visit.

Whatever the reason may be, however, one cannot approach theology in our time—or any other part of our lives, for that matter—without running head-on into the work of men like Jean-

François Lyotard, Michel Foucault, Ludwig Wittgenstein, Jacques Derrida, and some two or three dozen more philosophers of stature, including existential thinkers like Albert Camus and Jean-Paul Sartre.

While, with the probable exception of Camus and Sartre, the names of our recent philosophers may not be generally familiar, the consequences of their professional lives very much are. From the perspective of our interests here, they have impacted Emergence Christianity in two ways. The first of these is as circular as is the proverbial cat chasing its own tail.

As the works of the twentieth-century philosophers began to deconstruct all written texts and to challenge the ability of language to convey anything without prejudice, so too, as we have noted, came a growing anxiety, especially among younger Emergences, about seminary training. Emergence distrust of, and hesitancy about, institutionally based and/or academically brokered theology was and is, in its sensibilities, not unlike that which Charles Parham had first expressed in the years preceding Azusa Street, but it is more informed. That is, there was and is the very real fear that formal training in academic theology might somehow entrap one in a spiritual and intellectual prison constructed of words that, obviously, themselves were built upon and around and out of other words that were themselves rooted in other words that were based upon . . . et cetera, ad infinitum. The other troubling thing was the realization that the metaphorical prison was patrolled by very real professors and credentialed scholars, almost all of whom had vested professional interests in seeing that the words particular to their own theological or scholarly bent were the words accepted.

The cat-with-its-tail part of this is that, lacking faith in institutionalized theological training, many leaders and thinkers within Emergence Christianity turned to secular institutions for their education. There they were exposed to and studied, among other things and by requirement, at least some contemporary philosophy.

Beyond that, many of them even ended up taking advanced work and advanced degrees in the very field that had used words and language to impugn the words and language of the seminary training they had rejected because of the untrustworthiness of unchallenged words, et cetera, ad infinitum. Irony is ever and always interesting, whether in cats or people.

Meta-Narrative

The other, two-pronged, and far more substantive consequence of the twentieth-century philosophers upon Emergence and, by extension, upon Emergence Christianity has been, first, the exposure to public view of the fallacies patent in our meta-narratives and, second, formal philosophy's assertion of the very real truth that no text is ever impervious to the influences of the context in which it was created and/or is received.

The "grand stories" or "big ideas" of the centuries between the Great Reformation and the Great Emergence were, without question or apology, the ones around which our forefathers and mothers constructed their lives. Thus, there was, for them, the absolute possibility of absolute freedom. Such was a God-given right and entirely achievable, or it would be if only they could live correctly and construct their polity correctly.

There was absolute time and only one reality. History was progress. Beyond question, humankind—especially Caucasian humankind—was on a linear trajectory. We were going somewhere better than that which had been when our ancestors lived, and children would always go farther than their progenitors had gone. The human story was a forward-thrusting record of an inevitable and unstoppable forward-thrusting creation.

We were coming to an age—stood on the very brink of it, in fact—when our kind could know everything about the universe, a time when everything in creation could be explained, everything broken down into its constituent parts (for all things were reducible to their parts), and when the articulation of those parts would at last be fully exposed to human understanding and benefit . . . myths, all myths. Myths that were life-giving or, at the very least, life-organizing in their time, but still myths . . . grand myths . . . meta-narratives.

So, it comes to be obvious for Emergences that meta-narratives must be suspect and, thus, that only micro-narratives are trustworthy. Only the little stories that admit the limitations of their genesis and their reach are of value. Some kind of grand scheme that explains it all and purports to give individual lives a resulting function and worth is not only incredible but also a destructive lie, except . . . except there is a Great Narrative that, for Christians of any and every era, has always been there. For the Christians of Emergence, however, that narrative has a defining, new grandeur. The understanding that undergirds that grandeur is, however, a bit difficult to articulate, much less to grasp at first.

Be-ing-ness

For Christians, God is. For many Emergence Christians, God Is-ing, for lack of a better way to state the matter. That is, God Is Being-ness or Is-ing-ness. God is—again for lack of a better term—a verb, an Event. "Say to them, 'I am,'" is, after all, the response to Moses's query about Who/What he should say was sending him out as prophet and leader. And, to the extent that some small part of the grandeur of Is-ing-ness or Be-ing-ness is recountable, then the tale told—i.e., the meta-narrative—is the story of God's Godness as it is caught within time and circumstance and as humanity, also caught within time and circumstance, is allowed to watch It at any given time.

Be-ing-ness cannot be defined, for it lies outside the range of human conceptual powers. (We cannot, in fact, even define "being" as it occurs within our own realm of reference.) The Grand Narrative of Be-ing-ness cannot, therefore, be either defined or confined. We who are extant in time and human circumstance are allowed to touch the Narrative, but never to assume it is only when and what we touch.

It is foolishness to think, as we have noted several times already, that any one characteristic or attitude or bit of theology like that above accrues to all of the myriad individuals who compose Emergence Christianity. Certainly the belabored business of trying to capture in words the uncapturable makes it patently clear that any attempt at uniformity or consensus of thought is a failed one before it even starts. Yet the result, despite all the variations of circumstances and modes of arrival, is, nonetheless, still fairly uniform. The result is that the Scripture stands, for most Emergence Christians, as a holy and living event.

Thus, to ask of a holy and living event that it be confined within the limitations of human comprehension, much less be captured within the fairly recent human concept of historicity, is to violate in every possible way the gift of glimpses that has been given. To reduce it to rules is not just to deny its scope and purposes but also to intentionally obscure and defile its consuming beauty.

The Basics

The Scripture may come to us already mediated, just as we ourselves will likewise mediate it. But its story—its integrity of story—is the sum of all its parts. And whether "factual" or not, the parts are all "actual." And for that reason, because of that one overarching, governing reason or mode of engagement, Emergence Christians, as a rule, may be said:

to be radically obedient to the words and teaching of the Christ as recorded in Scripture and as received, during discernment, prayer, and teachings, into their own beingness. At a practical level, there is a conjunctive application. There is the Emergence mantra of, "If you believe a thing, live it!" that both commands obedience and, by implication, decries a lot of talking about it.

to be insistent that there is only one story, not two stories in one set of covers. The so-called testaments are one Testament, and any engagement of one without full incorporation of the other is folly. There is, to this, also a concomitant respectful connection with Judaism and the Jewish people that has no historic analogue.[2]

to be willingly susceptible to the power and truth of story, but categorically suspicious of propositional truth and especially of doctrinal and/or dogmatic exegesis.[3]

to believe that theology as a conversation is something to be used as a means, not an end. As an inherited record of what others have thought, it is historically informing. As a contemporary statement of what others are thinking and/or receiving, it is an investigation of interest and worth. As a whetstone against which to sharpen one's own mind and concepts, it can be invaluable for what it can expose or suggest. But as an enshrined or fixed system for entering Scripture, it is most certainly something to be pushed out through and beyond, not entrenched within.

to opt always for grace over morality. "Micah 6:8 Christianity," a term one often hears these days, is a kind of bon mot for this stance. "What does the Lord require of you but to do justly, to love mercy, and to walk humbly with your God?" (NKJV).

to be entirely persuaded that orthopraxy, or right action, trumps orthodoxy, or right belief, every time, starting with the parables and their accounts of it in the Gospels.[4]

to know, above and beyond all else, that the Story tells us that there is a kingdom, that it is now and not yet, here and also

> there, fully come and coming and then, in knowing this, to live every minute of every day accordingly.

All that having been said, there are things other than a passionate engagement with Scripture that also inform Emergence Christianity and Emergence Christians. To enjoy a more nearly complete understanding of what, as a way of being and believing, it is and what, as a people, they are, we will need to look next at some of those other, albeit more loosely conjoined, things.

NOTES

1. Lest there be any confusion here, these words are mine and constitute no more than my own attempt at trying to summarize the contemporary circumstance as I have observed it to be.

2. This movement toward honoring Judaism, known as *philosemitism*, is as characteristic of Emergence citizens in general as it is of Emergence Christians in particular. Interested readers will want to see particularly the work of Professors Robert D. Putnam and David E. Campbell as presented in their magisterial volume, *American Grace* (Simon & Schuster, 2010).

3. One of the most profound, clear, and readable presentations of this position comes, as it logically should, from two Emergence Christian leaders. See *Free for All: Rediscovering the Bible in Community* by Emmaus Way pastors, Tim Conder and Daniel Rhodes (Baker, 2009).

One should also remember that it is in the area of propositional truth that the Emerging and the Emergent branches of Emergence differ most sharply, one from the other. The text's words here should be read with that distinction clearly in mind.

4. Brian McLaren has consistently been a clear and accessible explicator of this position. Interested readers will want to look in particular at his *A New Kind of Christianity* (HarperOne, 2010).

19

The Head and the Heart

Worshiping with Heart, Mind, Soul, and Strength

Emergence Christians approach their faith, logically enough, as Emergence citizens. Presumably, if that were not the case, they would have a different naming. But dwellers in Emergence they are, through and through; and like their fellow citizens, they by and large are dialogical in their pursuit of understanding; hospitable to a fault; decolonialized in their worldview, be it political or missional; antiauthoritarian in more than just their declericalization; enamored of paradox; demanding of authenticity as a prerequisite to any engagement of any sort; and, almost as a logical extension of authenticity, even more demanding that there be absolute transparency in whoever or whatever is. Unlike their fellow citizens of a more secular bent, however, Emergence Christians are both spiritual and religious.

There is an old and rather tired quip that holds that "the Great Reformation took Christianity north." What that refers to is not the transposition of the seats of theological power to Geneva and Scotland, but rather, it refers to the transposition of the center of faith from the human heart to the human head. Weary quip or not, those words still speak the truth.

Emergence Christians, in general and for better or for worse, tend to be more highly educated than are many of their fellow citizens. There is, in other words, no scorning among them of the head, the brain, and/or the mind. Indeed, those parts are all to be honored and utilized to the benefit of the whole of life. The use of mind in faithful living is not only to be desired, moreover, but it is actually to be understood as having been commanded in the words of our Lord, "Thou shalt love the Lord thy God with all thy heart, and with all thy soul, and with all thy mind, and with all thy strength."[1] There is also another and nuanced truth below the immediate surface of those words, however.

Whatever one does in employing the mind as an agency for loving God must be governed and assessed in terms of Jesus's full directive. That is, to love with the mind and its penchant for time-bound logic is good Christian practice only if the soul, heart, and spirit are privy in equal parts to the ongoing conversation. And in no part of Emergence Christian life is this understanding more visibly applied and present than it is in Emergence worship.

If there is diversity among Emergence Christians as groups within a grouping, there is infinitely more among them as worshipers. Services or worship or gatherings, or whatever term it is that is being used, always—always—involves music, but that music can run the gamut from electronica to Southern Gospel to superb jazz to Celtic laments to Christian rock to medieval chant and back again. Sometimes there is even a mix of it all within the confines of one grouping. Whatever the style or mix, however, the purpose is inevitably the same: to ensure that body, heart, and soul come as equals into the conversation.

What It Means to Be Incarnational

Christianity is a deeply incarnational religion. By that, one means, certainly, the principal belief that Jesus was God-in-Man and is

Man-in-God. But far more frequently in Emergence conversation, what is meant by "incarnational" is the understanding that the body and soul are inextricably bound. That is, there is within Emergence thought a kind of fierce assertion that Jesus walked around after the resurrection in a body and that that body, while it could pass through walls and enter sealed rooms, still had punctures in its hands from the nails of crucifixion and a hole in its side from the slash of a sword. It was also the body which ascended. We are bodies, and bodies we will ever be. In sum, to use Kester Brewin's rich phrasing, we are "wombs of the divine" and, God willing, always will be.[2]

As a result, every part of Emergence worship, from the music right down to the clapping and the swaying, is designed to be sure that bodies are in worship even as minds are to be likewise engaged. To further excite this totality of presence, every visual stimulus that is reasonably possible and productive of reverence is part and parcel of the worship experience. From dozens of candles to highly tactile fabrics like burlap and netting, from easels that invite the faithful to paint what they are hearing within themselves to screens and multiprojections of varying images, from potter's wheels that allow the mind to move through the fingers into the muddy stuff of life to the use of scented oils in anointing—all of it is there and every bit of it present because of one thing. All of the worshiper must be present for worship, profitable instruction, and godly discernment to occur. It is so commanded, and it must be so done.

Another Look at the Great Schism

Closely akin to the exercise of fully spiritualized incarnation and/or incarnated spirituality in all of life, and especially in worship, is an affinity for Orthodox praxis and, by extension, for Orthodox theology. As we have already noted earlier, there is always during our five-hundred-year upheavals a turning back to look, almost with nostalgia, at what was before it was so rudely interrupted by the coming of whatever it is that is being supplanted. It was entirely predictable and reasonable, then, that Emergence should jump back a thousand years to consider again what it was that the Great Schism of the eleventh century spirited away from those of us who are latinized Christians. Based on past history, that trip down memory lane would have happened regardless and then, shortly thereafter, it would have been essentially over and done with. But things were a bit different this time around.

Orthodoxy, of all the communions within Christianity, is the most sensual, the most keenly aesthetic, the most elegant and routinely mystical. In sum, it is the most incarnational in the sense of Emergence's use of that word and, thereby, the most spiritual as well as religious. One of the first signs of the rapid spread of Emergence Christianity in this country was not released in some demographer's facts and figures or even in media coverage of odd and peculiar worship groups. Rather, it was much humbler. It was in the spiking of sales in icons and incense and stoles.[3]

Emergences had found the older ways of the faith and they loved them—not "liked," for that would be too removed a word. No, they loved these signs and symbols and conveyers of nonverbal truth, these tools for being spiritual as well as religious in community and with candor.

There is another old quip—or it is as old as any commentary about Emergence can be—that says that Emergences love their icons, but are clueless about how either to read or to write one. The words may be humorous and the witticism wry, but one should be very cautious in declaring that Emergence Christians are clueless about much of anything, especially religion. Once again, their general penchant for learning and their somewhat greater levels of education both put the lie to that kind of jest; but at the same time, those very things also help to explain why Emergences are prone to be unfettered borrowers from, and shrewd adapters of, other traditions. That certainly has been the case with Orthodoxy.

While icons and candles may have been the first indicators of some rather substantial appropriation in progress, they were only the beginning of a much longer saga. Once Emergence thinking had entered into Orthodoxy via its overt signs and accoutrements, then questions about the ethos itself and the theology behind these new joys began to come into play as well.

Filioque

When the Great Schism occurred, it occurred across every part of the eleventh-century European, Middle Eastern, and North African world. It occurred as well because of a whole baker's dozen of economic, political, and cultural conflicts, but the symbolic straw that broke the camel's back—or better said, that broke the known world into shattered pieces—was a religious issue. It was the *filioque*.

Filioque, like "meta-narrative," is basically of no use until it is translated into contemporary language. Rendered literally from the Latin, it means "from the Son." And just as surely as Luther and Zwingli parted at Marburg Palace over the nature of the bread and wine, so surely did East and West break apart over "from the Son." And Emergence Christians are quite right when they say that latinized Christianity has never been the same since, for what we are really speaking of is an understanding or way of conceptualizing the nature and being of the Holy Spirit.

Orthodoxy holds, as it always has, that both God the Son and God the Holy Spirit descend from God the Father. Latinized Christianity holds, as it has vigorously and aggressively done since before the eleventh century, that God the Holy Spirit descends from God the Father *and* God the Son, thus, our *filioque*.

The result of the Great Schism, for the latinized Christianity in which the majority of Emergences grew up, has been an understanding of the Holy Spirit as somehow less than, or as the least of three, or as the vaguest and most uneasily defined of the named parts—or maybe, at least in popular lay imagination, as not really there at any independent level at all. Heresy to the Orthodox—heresy a thousand years ago, heresy today.[4]

But for Emergence Christians, as for the Renewalists from whom many of them come, there was Azusa Street, there was Bennett, there was Wimber, there was Spirit. And it is Spirit whom they engage as fully as they engage the Christ and/or the Father. Orthodoxy not only gives license to that, but it also provides the symbols and images to validate it.

Perichoresis

Just as important is the fact that both Orthodox theology and Orthodox icons—especially Andrei Rublev's writing of the Trinity—present a Trinity that is communal, one that is, in fact, a community of Its Parts. Orthodoxy, with its deep sense of incarnational theology and of the holy uses of beauty, has a name for this unity of perfection and balance.

Perichoresis is not a term one hears very often, if ever, in latinized Christian conversation, but it certainly occurs with frequency in Emergence conversation. It obviously is Greek, and we derive our word *choreography* from it. Knowing that correlation can help sometimes to elucidate what *perichoresis* is trying to name. As nearly as it can be brought into English, *perichoresis* is the perfect and harmonious being-together-ness of things and parts when they are in dance. And the Trinity, for Orthodox Christians, is unceasingly in *perichoresis* or is perichoretic. It is community at its most exquisite.

Emergences, whether secular or religious, are communal by culture and era. The affirmation, then, of a fully felt and experienced Trinity conceived as community makes experiential sense. It also tends, of course, to make other and different modes of understanding appear to be even more intellectualized and alien than might otherwise be the case.

And last but not least, a complete and fully communal Trinity gives license to an ecclesiology that is communal and community based . . . to an ecclesiology, in other words, that is as natural to Emergence as structured and segmented congregations are off-putting and sterile.

Apophatic vs. Kataphatic Theology

Orthodoxy has kindly lent Emergence several other benefits and blessings. One of them especially militates for our attention here, and that is the introduction of apophatic theology into some streams of the Emergence conversation.[5]

Apophatic theology is the approach to God and to describing God that speaks in terms of that which God is not. Kataphatic theology, its categorical opposite, has characterized latinized Christianity's approach for most of history and almost exclusively for the last half a millennium. While apophatic Christians laud God in terms of what God is not, kataphatic Christians understand and convey God in terms of what God is. Both streams of faith speak of God in terms of God's roles, of course. It is, rather, in their approach to the beingness of God that the two differ sharply.

Emergence Christians are, as we have seen, both culturally and educationally skittish of too much blind faith in words at any time. They are especially skittish around human beings who believe that they can reduce Godness to description and thereby convey what God is and what God thinks.

". . . *thinks*?" Already, you see, we have, by our very words, imposed on Beingness a human construct. Not good. Not good at all, and certainly not defensible. Or so say many Emergence Christians.

While it is incontestably true that one could walk into almost any Emergence gathering and, by using the word "apophatic," provoke a lot of confused frowns and shaking heads, it is still true that the thinking, attitudes, and religious prejudices hiding under that label are in plain view.[6] It is equally true that apophatic thinking leads straight to mysticism or, conversely, mysticism historically leads straight into apophatic thinking, and whatever else Emergence Christians are, they most surely do tend toward mysticism over absolutes and assertions.

Disciplines and Practices

Incarnational inclinations show themselves among Emergences in yet another way that we have already mentioned, but that needs expansion here in this context. The Abrahamic faiths of Judaism, Christianity, and Islam all hold in common the tradition of the ancient disciplines. Since "discipline" is less attractive as a word now than once it was, Emergences tend to speak of the seven as being ancient "practices." Either way, the seven function, as they have for millennia, as intentional habits of the mind, body, heart, and soul instituted for the express purpose of shaping an extant person into an observant believer.

Of the seven, three govern the body's senses and four govern or monitor human time. The body is most sustained (and, aside from sexual activity, most gratified) by food. Therefore, the withholding of food in sacred fasts and the celebration of food in the sacred meal call the body's attention regularly to its function as part of a worshiping integer or whole.

Beyond fasting and celebratory eating, the body rejoices in its work and measures its success in work in terms of the resulting products, whether they are monetary or material. Taking one-tenth of that proof and returning it to the divine both teaches the believer the virtues of thanksgiving and sharing, and also trains the body always to remember for whom and through whom and toward whom it works.

As for the four that monitor human time, the keeping of the daily offices—or of fixed-hour prayer, if one prefers that terminology—is the first. It monitors the individual day by returning the believer every three hours to the business of praise and spiritual intercourse with the holy. The second, which is the keeping of Sabbath, monitors the next largest unit of human time, the human week. In the keeping of Sabbath, the believer does as the Creator did by resting, certainly, but there is also a subtler component. By interrupting the work of life on a regular basis, the believer comes to understand that success in that work depends from God, not from unremitting human effort.

The still larger temporal unit of the human year is monitored not only by the physical calendar that accrues to all people but also by the observance of the liturgical year in which each part of the faith's story is remembered, reviewed, reverenced, and often reenacted. The largest unit in human time, that of a complete life with all its accumulation of years, is marked or honored by pilgrimage.

Like the spiking of sales for candles and icons, so the remarkable spiking of sales in the late 1990s of books for keeping fixed-hour prayer and for observing Sabbath furnished the first documentable indications of just how completely the spiritual disciplines or practices were being inculcated into Emergence Christian lives. The inclusion in Emergence services of the Eucharist is now standard operating procedure for most. The business of building worship around, and of dressing worship space in terms of, the liturgical year is essentially ubiquitous, and fasting is mentioned more often than would have been true even fifteen years ago. Pilgrimage remains as the least observed of the seven, though thanks to Iona and Taizé that too is changing.

Of the seven practices, it is tithing that, interestingly enough, gets the least play both in general Emergence conversation and in

Emergence teachings specifically. There are probably at least two good reasons for that, the first being clearly reactionary. Tithing and Sabbath observance were the two practices that not only survived the Reformation's cutting board but also lived on to become exercises urged unceasingly and sometimes mercilessly upon the reformed faithful. Especially where tithing is concerned, the strong odor of institutional self-interest as opposed to pastoral concern for spiritual formation is still sufficient reason to give most Emergences pause. Beyond that and far more laudably, Emergence leaders take the position—and frequently state it—that "collections" or "offerings," while they are routinely taken up, should be seen first as a responsibility of the community and not of its visitors or observers and, second, that supporting financially with the product of one's labors is indeed a spiritual exercise, long before it is a fiscal one. Contributing should be done, then, only from that motivation and only in concord with what the Spirit directs. Laudable, indeed.[7]

NOTES

1. Mark 12:30 KJV.
2. *Signs of Emergence*, 94.
3. During the 1990s, when these spikes began to show up in commercial sales reports, most products of this kind moved through religion bookstores rather than through gift and specialty shops. As a result, the book industry was aware of the shift earlier than were some other segments of the retailing industry. For religion book publishers, the spikes came as welcome—and accurate!—harbingers of things to come.
4. Always there are treacherous spots when one is treating of religion, and this is an especially dangerous one. It is important, therefore, that clarity accrue. In every bitter religious severance, what one side of the argument calls heresy, another calls sacred doctrine. There is no intention here to resolve that tension nor to attempt to establish the rightness or wrongness of either side in the *filioque* argument. What matters for our purposes here is that we perceive the history and attitudes that explain the presence of apophatic thought as a functioning line of thought within Emergence Christianity.
5. This approach of discovering the positive by engaging the negative is not entirely missing from latinized Christian experience. It usually presents as *via negativa* and almost always within communities and eras interested in mysticism. One especially finds mention and even practice of it within medieval Latin Christianity.

6. The most delightful and also most instructive presentation of this is *How (Not) to Speak of God* by Peter Rollins (Paraclete Press, 2006). McLaren himself lauds it as "one of the most important contributions" to be made to the conversation as well as "one of the two or three most rewarding books of theology I have read in ten years." Strong words from a legendary leader.

On the other hand and because there is not unanimity of opinion on this, interested readers should read "Thy Kingdom Come (on Earth)," an essay by Kevin Corcoran in the volume *Church in the Present Tense: A Candid Look at What's Emerging*, which he edited (Brazos, 2011). Corcoran elucidates with vigor and clarity the objections that some Emergences raise to the increasing presence of apophaticism in Emergence conversation.

7. One other important thing needs saying here. That is, we need to note once again that any abbreviated summary always runs the risk of error by omission. More disastrously, a summary like this one can run the risk of error by unintended implication. Lest that happen here, especially where the business of credentialed and/or academic theologians and institutionalized theology is concerned, we need to acknowledge, at least in passing, that Emergence Christianity has been shaped and informed by many brilliant theologians. Beyond that, Emergence leaders and pastors, whether seminary-trained or seminary-skittish, are in constant and intentional contact with many living theologians and professional philosophers, as well as with the work of many of those who are no longer living.

In this regard, Jürgen Moltmann has been an especially informing and influential presence, as has Miroslav Volf. We have already mentioned the influence of Lesslie Newbigin upon the Emergence conversation, just as the work of Roman theologians, especially that of Karl Rahner and David Tracy, has been seminal. Beatrice Bruteau and Philip Clayton, both academic philosophers, have helped shape the dialogue, and the impact of the Slovenian philosopher Slavoj Zizek is inestimable. The works of Lutheran theologian George Lindbeck, of the Methodist iconoclastic Stanley Hauerwas, and of the much-loved UCC theologian Walter Brueggemann have been influential at all three levels of lay, pastoral, and scholarly formation. The same thing has most surely and dramatically been true of the Anglican theologian and former bishop N. T. Wright, and his work. And the list goes on. . . .

To assume, then, that one can hope to understand Emergence Christianity without some modicum of familiarity with the work and welcomed instruction of these professionals would be tantamount to its own kind of heresy, and that is an error none of us can afford in these first, young years of Emergence Christianity's story.

Part 4

And Now What?

Thoughts on the Decisions and Dilemmas to Come

20

Reconfigure, Adapt, Realign

How Do the New and Old Fit Together?

The Great Emergence, as we know, is sometimes referred to as "the fifth turning" in recognition of the fact that ours is indeed the fifth time that latinized culture, and latinized Christianity with it, have gone through a time of enormous upheaval affecting every part of life and governance, faith, and belief. While each of those times of tsunami-like transition has been distinct unto itself, each of them has also shared certain recurring similarities with its predecessors. There is, in other words, a kind of pattern that always asserts itself, even in the midst of all the other era-specific disruptions going on around it.

Mergers and Reconfigurations

One of the more obvious and inviolate subplots in this patterning is the fact, first, that whatever form of the faith had held hegemony or pride of place over the previous five hundred years has to drop back and give way. Second, it must, as part of that dropping back, reconfigure itself in order to survive and even to thrive. Orthodoxy did not cease to be after the Great Schism. Roman Catholicism did not cease to be after the Great Reformation. And Protestantism will not cease to be as a result of the Great Emergence. It will, however, have to reconfigure and adapt. In fact, it has already begun to do so, and the consequences of those adjustments and accommodations will affect Emergence Christianity just as surely and inevitably as they will affect established Christianity itself.

Evidences of such realignments have been present within Protestantism in this country for several decades. The creation of the "United" Methodist Church, the reconfiguration of one segment of Lutheranism into the Evangelical Lutheran Church in America, the forming of the United Churches of Christ, the rejoining of Presbyterian bodies into the Presbyterian Church in the United States all speak to this process.

Making even more noise, especially in this country, are mergers and reconfigurations and accommodations like that of the Called to Common Mission alliance. It was years in the making, for its purpose was to allow for, and then enable, full and free exchange of pastoral and ecclesial offices between the Evangelical Lutheran Church in America and the Episcopal Church of the United States. Such would have been unthinkable even as recently as the 1970s or '80s. Dwindling parishes, aging congregants, and a surplus of unoccupied real estate militated, however, over former niceties of theology and doctrine.[1] The result is exactly as originally intended: merged congregations in some places, Lutheran pastors in some Episcopal naves and vice versa, apostolic succession reconsidered, etc. But the real noise, if by that one means media coverage, began in 2011.

On April 14, 2011, for the first time in United States history, regional and mid-judicatories of the Moravian Church, the Evangelical Lutheran Church, and the Episcopal Church, in common worship, celebrated their full communion, one with another. Over two hundred clergy from the three bodies gathered in the Cathedral Church of the Nativity in Bethlehem, Pennsylvania, to renew their ordination vows before one another and to give reverence, each to the other, to the vows of all present without regard to former denominational boundaries. The press had a field day, or at least a pleasant picnic. A new day had indeed dawned.

Growth

That new day has shown up in some other ways as well. By 2010, the Barna Group, based on its then current surveys and data, was estimating "that by the end of the next decade 40 percent of all church-attending Christians will be worshipping God outside the parameters of a traditional congregational context."[2] What at first blush might seem to be a message of doom and gloom for established latinized Christianity was not. At least, not necessarily so. Quite the contrary, in fact, because once again we stumble across the truth that Hyphenateds are a new kind of congregants for this new day.

At the same time that the Barna Group was giving their careful and best assessment of the size and direction of Emergence, other figures began to come in showing that there was the beginning of a small growth in numbers in the Church of England. A miracle? If so, why? How? Such ran counter to everything one would have been led to expect, except . . .

. . . except the Church of England had been at the business of Hyphenateds and Fresh Expressions longer than had any other established body in latinized Christianity. And what was growing was not the parishes that had only the traditional Sunday worship services. What was growing were the kirk-and-chick parishes, and it was definitely the chicks who were doing the growing.

The question then arises about whether or not those whose names appear on St. Whoever's rolls by virtue of their participation in an off-site and entirely different, but still affiliated and maintained, form of worship are really Anglicans? And the only answer to that is a perfectly good Emergence one. The answer is yes and no. They are Hyphenateds, though what they are to become and what their impact on the church universal will be is anybody's guess at this point.

Progressive Christianity

Not all of established or traditional Protestantism has been quite so agile, of course, and there will undoubtedly be some feathering away of some of its more familiar pieces. In fact, there probably already is. One of the recurring questions within Protestantism over recent years has been about the role and future of Progressive Christianity and, even, about whether or not that term had any validity or descriptive power anymore.

In 2010, on his blog, *A Peculiar Prophet*, William H. Willimon, a much-quoted Methodist bishop and theologian, made his own assessment of that question quite clear:

> The pastoral ministry in mainline Protestantism will need to find a theological way through the intellectual death of theological liberalism (Progressive Christianity) and the cultural compromises of traditional evangelicalism.[3]

Some eighteen months later, *Patheos*, the online journal for Progressive Christianity, ran a series of postings in which they asked both Progressive and Emergence leaders and thinkers to address the question of whether or not those who call themselves "Progressives" still have a meaningful place as a part or segment of traditional Christianity or are, instead, a representation of Emergence still burdened with a totally un-Emergence kind of label and way of operating.

If the answer to the latter is yes, then the gradual merging of a part of Progressives and Progressive Christian structure back into the mainline from which it came and the merging of other parts of it into Emergence Christianity and Emergence structures will be formative and, one would hope, blessed as well. Like the Hyphenateds, Progressives—or former Progressives, as the case might be—could become welcome lines of communication between what was and what is becoming as the two work in common cause for the kingdom on earth.

While there was no consensus amongst the *Patheos* writers or, presumably, among their readers, about exactly where Progressive Christianity might be going, there is a fairly clear consensus that Bishop Willimon was correct in naming evangelicalism as the theological Charybdis to Progressive Christianity's Scylla. Over several months in 2010, *Christianity Today*, the journal of evangelicalism in the United States, ran a series of what it called "Global Conversations" about the state of evangelicalism worldwide. The last conversation was specifically about the business of reconfiguring in the face of a new Reformation. Titling the print report of the conversation as "A 21st Century Reformation," *Christianity Today* asked an evangelical leader from Malaysia, one from Argentina, one from Nigeria, and a fourth, Dr. Leighton Ford from this country, to respond to the following question:

> The Reformation of the 16th century was a revolution of mythic proportions. Scholars and pastors with fresh spiritual insights took advantage of revolutionary changes in the arts, science, humanities, politics, travel, and commerce to turn the Western world upside down. It marked both a return to biblical roots and a leap into the future. In the 21st century, what major changes in the church should Christians be hoping and working for?

Dr. Ford's answer, while it was a mini-essay of sorts, called especially for what, borrowing from McLaren, he called "a generous evangelism."[4] As is his wont, he was very correct about what would be required and very predictive of what might not happen.

Evangelicalism

Evangelicalism is not going to cease to exist in the face of Emergence any more than Protestantism is, though the two bodies are hardly analogous, one being less a defined organization and more a mind-set or ethos than is the other. But by 2011, it was apparent that evangelicalism, which had already been in a state of internal tensions and unease for at least a quarter century, was suffering what might become a splitting of itself into two or perhaps three parts.

Books are peculiar things. As inoffensive-looking items of little size or weight, they can unleash forces that outdo hurricanes for blast and destruction. Like hurricanes, of course, they also have to come at precisely the right time and into the precisely right set of circumstances to do that. In 2011, when Rob Bell, former teaching pastor of the Emergent Mars Hill Church in Grand Rapids and an Emergence leader internationally, released a small, innocent-looking book entitled *Love Wins*, he in effect released a hurricane.

One suspects that such was hardly Bell's original purpose, much less his desire. The amusing thing about the whole brouhaha, in fact—assuming that anything could legitimately be seen as amusing in all the uproar—was that professional book critics made the point over and over again that there are few if any "positions" or "doctrinal stances" in the whole volume. *Love Wins* is, fundamentally, a form of apophatic theology. It asks questions as a way of discussing the unanswerable. It's just that the questions being asked sat right in the middle of evangelicalism's most vulnerable spots, right in the middle of paradox and even of inconsistencies in Scripture concerning eschatology, the nature of the afterlife, and Christian exclusivity. It was not, in other words, *Love Wins* that, in and of itself, triggered such a storm of conversation by virtue of what Bell said so much as it was a matter of the time and circumstances of his saying them.

For at least two decades before *Love Wins*, evangelicals and Christians of evangelical persuasions had managed to avoid having to engage directly the concerns of many of their non-evangelical coreligionists. In a host of non-evangelical minds, both clerical and lay, there had been the contained but pervading sense that some of Scripture speaks to universal salvation, not Christian particularity, and that descriptions and dogmas concerning hell had perhaps been more decorated and elaborated by the faithful than should have been the case. With the coming of *Love Wins*, those unpleasant but still intermural problems suddenly were no longer containable. They also ceased to be unpleasant and became pathologic. They became the line in the sand. Cross it, and you are no longer an evangelical.[5]

Since that time, the conflicts within evangelicalism and those between it and Emergence Christianity have become fiercely apparent. Over the coming years, some evangelicals will undoubtedly return fully to mainline traditions. Some will remain true to a numerically smaller and less influential evangelicalism. Many, in pursuit of Ford's generous evangelism, will join Emergence groups and gatherings where, predictably, they will bring not only dedication and energy but quite possibly a more politicized sensibility and praxis, a circumstance that could prove interesting, to say the least.

New Calvinism

In all of the reconfiguring and adjusting and accommodating that is happening within the church in response to the increasingly perceived and felt presence of Emergence Christianity, there is one other response that must command our attention. Before we move on to some of the questions Emergence Christianity must answer and some of the problems it must soon solve, we must at least tip our collective hats to the New Calvinism.

Just as, in our times of upheavals, there is always a regrouping and reconfiguring on the part of what has been in order to accommodate for changed circumstances and new players, so too there is always what we labeled earlier as a serious push-back. While push-back often sounds to us nowadays like a negative thing, it is not always so. In fact, in the case of the Great Emergence, history may say of at least one of our elicited "push-backs" that it was a beneficial thing for the church in several of its parts and presentations.

John Calvin was eight years old when Luther tacked his Ninety-Five Theses up for all to see. Yet the Christianity coming out of the Great Reformation was to be as shaped by Calvin as it was by Luther. Now, five hundred years later, Calvin is once again shaping a segment of Christianity, this time in response to the Great Emergence. Or if Calvin himself cannot be said to be doing the shaping, then most certainly his theology, ecclesiology, and philosophy can be.

This "New Calvinism" is not a product of any standing branch of established Protestantism, and certainly not of Presbyterianism, per se. Nor is it limited to, or confined by, the structure and praxis of any established body, though it may sometimes still carry the name of one.[6] But then, neither is it Emergence Christianity in the same way that Simple Church is or Neo-monastics are or—interestingly enough—not even as Hyphenateds are. It is composed, nonetheless, of Christians and worshipers who are citizens of the Great Emergence. Most of them are, in fact, fairly young to mid-career professionals and, consequently, share the sensibilities and predilections of Emergence living. The resulting construct created from all of this is both a push-back against what is on the part of those who are in it, and also an integer unique unto itself. That same construct is, moreover, one of the—perhaps *the*—most rapidly growing segments of Christianity in this country today.

There is, historically, an affinity between America and Calvinism, for Calvin's teachings furnished the intellectual foundation for both democracy and open-market capitalism as they came to be practiced in this country. In addition to that comfort zone of cultural familiarity, the austerity or antimaterialism of Calvin's thought appeals greatly to those who, living in a bizarre richness of goods and opportunity, are very fearful of the spiritual burden and shackling that come with possessions and opulence.

This New Calvinism, like the original it draws from, believes in sin and is quite willing to speak about it publicly. It is confessional, seeing humility and candor and repentance as necessary parts of Christian growth and absolutely requisite for the forming of Christian community. To the New Calvinists, Sweet Jesus, your Cosmic Hero and Dearest Friend, is as disgusting—and dangerous—a bit of pseudo-theology as has ever been invented. The emphasis on family, on solidarity in marriage and the bearing and rearing of children, is enormous. So, too, and concomitantly, is the emphasis on Scripture teaching and formation within the home as well as within the gathered body.

None of this is new, of course, but neither is it revival. Rather, it is, as we have said, push-back. It is the application of one integrated body of orthodox, latinized Christian teaching to Great Emergence circumstances. It is a resistance to Emergence Christianity in many ways, while at the same time sharing Emergence's etiology and essence. As such and because of its sheer size, it will also be a participant in, or at the very least a potent influence upon, the events and decisions that, during the coming decades, will determine the shape of Emergence Christianity in its full maturity.

NOTES

1. While this list of woes can sometimes seem so familiar and so oft bandied about as to be trite, it is far from it. By 2009, *Christian Century* was running figures showing that 59 percent of the congregants in old-line Protestantism in

this country were over sixty-five (October 6, 2009). Within a year after that, the Episcopal Church USA in 2010 was closing three parishes a month within its communion. Theology does indeed pale in the face of such.

2. As taken from the British magazine *CHRISTIANITY* (April 2011, p. 53). The same magazine, on page 15, also, editorially, attributes the Church of England growth to parishes with fresh expressions components. In this regard, see as well Paul Woolley, "The Challenge to Secularisation," *CHRISTIANITY*, November 2010, 17.

3. Bishop Will Willimon, "Ten Theses about the Future of Ministry," *A Peculiar Prophet*, April 24, 2010, http://willimon.blogspot.com.

4. Leighton Ford, "A 21st Century Reformation: Be Agents of Reconciliation," *Christianity Today*, September 2010, 32–35.

5. Some of the most enlightening of the contemporary commentary about these events and their consequences can be found in Jimmy Spencer's posting, "Love Wins: A Split in Protestant Evangelicalism" (March 14, 2011), on Tony Campolo's blog, *Red Letter Christians*, and in Scot McKnight's continuation of Spencer's commentary on his own *Jesus Creed* blog. They may be found, respectively, at http://www.redletterchristians.org/love-wins-a-new-split-in-protestant-evangelicalism/ and http://www.patheos.com/blogs/jesuscreed/2011/03/18/a-tipping-point/.

6. Three of the largest New Calvinist bodies in this country do still carry denominational names and, to some greater or looser extent, denominational connections. Anyone wishing to become acquainted with the New Calvinism as it functions on the ground here could do no better than to take a look at Capitol Hill Baptist Church in Washington, DC, or John Piper's Bethlehem Baptist Church in Minneapolis, or perhaps best-known of them all, Tim Keller's Redeemer Presbyterian in New York, and Mark Driscoll's whole network of Acts 29 congregations scattered across the country.

21

Where Now Is Our Authority?

Questioning and Establishing a Credible Voice

The chief characteristic of all the five-hundred-year upheavals that beset latinized Christian culture is—and always has been—the disestablishment of whatever source or definition of authority has been operative. That unseating of what has been is always followed, naturally enough, by the raising of the resulting question, "Where now is our authority?" or put another way, "How now shall we live? By whose rules? Under what definitions of the Good and the Worthy?"

For the centuries between the Great Schism and the Great Reformation, the pope, along with his curia and magisterium, was the ultimate source of authority. And if there were ever to be a reformation of any kind, they, and His Holiness along with them, had to be dethroned. Accordingly, Luther and his colleagues set about the business of Rome's disestablishment with fervor and, ultimately, with success. That success, though, left a hollow chamber in which the "Where now is our authority?" question reverberated with distressing constancy.

Scripture Only

It is a familiar story, of course, one we have even referenced earlier in this volume. It, nonetheless, needs revisiting. Eventually, Luther answered the authority problem—or the problem of an authority gone missing—by affirming Scripture as the only base on which human business and values and life could be built and by which they were to be governed. What Luther established as *sola scriptura, scriptura sola*—only the Scripture and the Scripture only—morphed its way, over the subsequent centuries, into becoming what is now known as the doctrine or principle of Protestant Inerrancy, the belief that the Bible is subject to historicity, that it is, in other words, an infallible, internally consistent, and historically accurate recounting of facts.

As an authority for valuing and governing latinized life, the inerrant Bible held sway until the opening days of the peri-Emergence in the middle of the nineteenth century. From those early years in the 1840s until the closing ones of the twentieth century, the task of disestablishing Luther's solution of *sola scriptura* was in full swing. And by the turn of the millennium, it had been completed in many parts of Christendom. Where now is our authority?

Protestant Inerrancy

Just as Luther's disestablishment of Rome put the question of authority squarely in the hands of the Reformers for answering, so the disestablishment of Protestant Inerrancy has put the question squarely in the hands of Great Emergence citizens, leaders, and theologians. The difference this time, as we know, is that we are once again living in an era of double, and now triple, citizenship. The answer to the authority question this time around will have to be, as it was two thousand years ago, different in its secular presentations than it is in its sacred one.

If that be the case—and it is—then Emergence Christianity, hopefully in conjunction with other communions within the faith, is free to discover and acknowledge an authority based not on Christendom but on the paradigm of the kingdom of God on earth. At the same time, however, it must also discover and acknowledge an authority, if possible, that provides for Christians a peaceful cohabitation with the political or secular authority that frames their physical life . . . all of which will welcome Emergence Christians into a tension that has long been familiar to our fellow Abrahamics, Judaism and Islam.

Just as surely as the question of the dislocation and then relocation of authority comes into play during every semi-millennial event, so too do two, and sometimes three, other signatory questions that also arise and then wait, somewhat impatiently, for their time in the sun. The easiest—ironically said, because it most surely is in no way "easy," just "easier"—the easiest, most direct and addressable of the three questions staring twenty-first-century Christians, both Emergence and otherwise, in the face is that of our need for a theology of both ecclesiology and religion.

The Role of Ecclesiology

For centuries, the church operated—and much of it still operates—under the principle of *extra ecclesiam nulla salus*: aside from or apart from the church, there is no salvation. Is that true? Still true? Ever true? If so, what is the church? If not, what is its function? In either case, how is it to be in an Emergence culture?

Is Christianity the only way? How does one resolve the apparent contradiction between "No man cometh unto the Father, but by me" and "Unless you eat the flesh of the Son of Man and drink his blood, you have no life in you" with words like "I have other sheep that are not of this fold" or "In My Father's house are many mansions; if it were not so, I would have told you"?

In our times of dual and triple citizenship, how can one live as a devout, missional, practicing Christian in a civil polity made up of devout, missional, and practicing members of other, and often antithetical, faiths? How can one do that responsibly without either creating civil unrest and strife or else curbing the full expression and exercise of faith?

The questions mount up, all of them but variations on a theme, and the theme is, "How now are we to understand religion? What is its place in human salvation?"

The reentry of Islam into latinized Christian culture has certainly lent to those questions an immediacy and intensification that cannot be either ignored or denied, especially in Europe.[1] But that urgency is only the surface presentation of the deeper question that is, indeed, one of foundational Christian doctrine: What is our theology about religion and religions? We do not know, and if history repeats itself this time as it has in the past, it will be Emergence Christianity that leads the search for an answer.

Citizens of the Great Emergence, whether Emergence Christians or otherwise, also face together another question, this one so unprecedented that concern with developing a credible theology of religion pales before it. For the first time in human history, so far as anyone can ascertain, we do not know what a human being is. We, as a species, have a treasure trove of literature and philosophy from many cultures dealing with the "Who am I?" question, but nothing that even approximates an answer to the "What are we?" one. Arguably, in fact, there has never before been any need for that question to arise, much less any frame of reference for it to come up out of. Enter the Great Emergence.

Or perhaps, enter the peri-Emergence, for the roots of our confusion go as far back as Mesmer and Freud in the nineteenth century when science first began to probe the human interior to discover what that cavernous space contains and who inhabits it. Their work was passed on to men like William James and Carl

Jung and the birthing of psychology as a major discipline and, from that matrix, into a panoply of related disciplines as diverse as cognitive science and neurobiology. But it was in the middle of the twentieth century that our confusion about what we are became too apparent to ignore.

For centuries, humanity had defined itself as distinct from the rest of creation by virtue of its ability to think. The biological sciences of the twentieth century rather quickly established the fact that animals also "think," if by that one means the ability to remember, to anticipate, to congregate, to mourn, to learn, to create rituals, and to problem-solve. Given those unsettling discoveries, the definition of humanness became the presence of an autobiographical self along with a conscious awareness of it. For the Christian especially, trained as we are to understand ourselves as created in the image of God—in *imago dei*—this was a happy solution right up until two or three things became obvious, even to the person on the street.

The fact that people with multiple personalities have more than one autobiographic self has always been a bit troubling, of course, but that problem was as nothing compared to the fact that the drug age, for all of its horrors, also opened up to full view the fact that the "person" inside could be "changed" in much the way one changes clothes, from personality or integer A to person or personality B and back again. It would appear, in other words, that consciousness is a construct of the mind that is the perceptualizing function of the brain that is controlled and ordered by whatever chemical wash bathes its neurons and synapses.

If we are not our consciousness, what are we? If in our being-ness we are simply the result of chemical caprice, then where is *imago dei*? What, then, is the soul and where does it dwell?

The questions have mounted in number, of course, with the exponential growth of computer science and all it has taught us about thinking processes and now, even, about emotive ones. The merging of humanity with machines, benign at first, increasingly confuses the issue of which part is which, or is there a new unity, a cyborg, to use the current term. What of robots? As we now employ them in warfare, they are things, but when does the thingness wash over into something else, and what would that something else be? We don't know, but we do know that transhumanism is now a broad area of scholarly and clinical and legal study.

The tendency is to shrug these questions off as being too rarefied or ethereal as to have any impact, except of course that, whether ignored or not, they chew away at every part of Emergence culture. The Terry Schiavo story still stands as a sorrowful example of Emergence inability to define what is and is not a life. The abortion wars, now of some fifty years standing, bear unremitting witness to an abiding lack of clarity about what is and is not a human being. Like it or not, penal codes, systems of punishment, sentencing to corrective therapy—they all must depend from some understanding of what a human being is and how responsible and/or malleable.

We watch Watson win at *Jeopardy!* and even as we chuckle, we feel another bit of our domain erode beneath us. We understand that, since 1953 with the coming of molecular genetics and the discovery of the double-helix in DNA, our "us-ness" has become subject to external manipulation. It has become so much so, in fact, that now a goodly portion of the human genome is owned and patented by corporations, most of them pharmaceutical. What, then, are the implications of bioengineering, for that clearly is the motivation behind "owning" a part of the code that structures us?

And it does indeed go on and on and on until we come at last to the realization that we, as a culture, must find some definition of humanness that informs accurately these new understandings about who we and our kind really are. Beyond that for Christians, the greater realization is that we have temporarily lost clarity about *imago dei* and, by extension, of the soul. Both those circumstances must be resolved, again hopefully by all Christian communions in concert. Either way, it is still true that Emergence Christianity, more than all the others, cannot avoid them.

Atonement

For Emergence Christians, there is another unavoidable question as well, and it is the bitterest—or at least the most divisive—of them all. Emergence Christianity, like all the previous communions that have come into being, must struggle with the atonement—or more properly, with the nature of the atonement.

Christianity, in its early days, had no theory of the atonement or of its mechanics; or if it did, there is no written record left to bear witness to that fact. Rather, it is with the coming of St. Augustine and his doctrine of original sin in the late fourth and early fifth centuries that Christian theologians began to wrestle with the question of why exactly the Son of God had to die in any way, but certainly in such a horrible, demeaning, and excruciating way.

Over the years since Augustine, there have been at least seven distinctly different answers to that question, the most recent of them being the Protestant one of substitutionary atonement, or more specifically, of penal substitution. According to that understanding, Jesus of Nazareth willingly accepted such punishment and death in order that He might become a living sacrifice or propitiation and thereby make it possible for a just God still, with integrity, to forgive the sins and offenses of His creatures.

For Emergence Christians—and here there is more unanimity than in some other areas of belief—the concept of an omnipotent and omniscient God who could find no better solution than that to the problem of sin is a contradiction of the first order. Even more repugnant is the notion that, if penal substitution as it is popularly and colloquially understood today is indeed the correct understanding of what happened at Calvary, then Christians are asked to accept as Father a God who killed His only child. Others of the penal substitution persuasion would hasten to say it was not God's child whom God sacrificed so much as God's self. In other words, once the verdict was in, the judge, in this case *the Judge*, not the guilty, bore the sentence. Unfortunately such nuances are lost on many, who are left with God as cosmic child abuser. Not reasonable and/or acceptable, say Emergent Christians, and the problem must be with the doctrine, not the Almighty. So where to start? Perhaps with original sin? But to do that invites the scandal and the burden of creating a whole new scheme, for the atonement, like it or not, is the linchpin in latinized Christian theology.[2]

Orthodoxy, lacking an Augustine, has never had latinized Christianity's understanding of the atonement. Rather it has held that incarnation was always God's intention from the beginning—from the Garden itself—and most certainly was not a reaction to the fall that happened in that Garden. As a result, substitutionary conversation in any form is in error. Principally, what Orthodoxy sees in the crucifixion is love unbounded and beyond all-knowing, love to be praised and worshiped and emulated to the salvation of creation itself.

Whether or not Emergence Christianity will once more borrow from Orthodoxy and thereby merge it even more tightly into the latinized experience of the faith is an open question, but the chances are that any astute gambler would probably lay money on "yes" as the more likely answer to that one.

NOTES

1. The Barnabas Fund, a United Kingdom–based Christian organization, released in February of 2011 a booklet entitled *Slippery Slope: Islamisation of the UK* by Patrick Sookhdeo. Despite its title, the fifty-page booklet, which is the print report of Barnabas's Operation Nehemiah, includes figures from other parts of Europe as well as from the United Kingdom. Evenhanded in its reportage, *Slippery Slope* offers very clear insight into the shifting demographics and religion-based tensions within European countries and should be a required, as well as an informing, read for both Christians and Muslims.

2. At the risk of becoming tedious about the whole thing, it must still be said that the basic offense of *Love Wins* and the core of the fury was about atonement, especially among evangelical Christians regardless of denominational affiliation. Interested readers will want to see, for instance, Mark Galli's review of Bell's book on p. 64ff. of the April 2011 edition of *Christianity Today*. As Galli notes, Bell "treats substitutionary atonement as culturally anachronistic." That would be very much an Emergence Christian stance on the part of an Emergence Christian.

22

Future Pressure

What Potential Struggles Await?

What is the future of religion? People frequently ask me this question, and I always want to respond like Dr. McCoy in *Star Trek*: "I'm a historian, not a fortune teller."[1]

The words are those of scholar and historian Diana Butler Bass, but the sentiment is almost universal among those who study contemporary religion. Perhaps the best way to speak predictively in any useful way, then, is to divide the question into two parts. What currently visible and very specific situations and issues can we identify as being those that will shape the immediate future of Emergence Christianity? And what can we identify as the sensibilities and circumstances that in all likelihood will shape its courses over the coming decades?

Power Struggles

Each question, even as a half of the larger one, is so vast as to require a book-length treatment in and of itself. For our purposes here, though, it is possible to pinpoint some of the more obvious current pressures upon Emergence Christianity, a goodly number of which have to do, in one way or another, with the problem of organization and structure. We know from thermodynamics, if nothing else, that there is no such thing as perfect order or perfect freedom. But where and how Emergence will find an orderly mode of being compatible with its nonhierarchal ways is a good question. It also is one that will not wait much longer for answering.

In a posting entitled "Inventive Church" on the Emergent Village weblog, Mike Stavlund described Common Table, the Emergence gathering where he worships and serves as teaching member, as "a unique sandbox in which we play." But then, much more soberly and sorrowfully, he went on to say that "there are occasional power struggles, which tend to be protracted because everyone is carefully insisting that there are no real power struggles." Stavlund, who is an influential voice in Emergence Christianity at large, spoke as well of an "ongoing, low-grade worry that comes with never being quite sure what is coming next year, next month, or even next week."[2]

Those concerns, which are certainly not idle ones, find their roots planted deep into the soil of Emergence itself and of its way of looking at the world. But Stavlund is correct in saying that they must be addressed, and very soon—addressed and, of course, resolved.

Closely akin to the matter of discovering a form of organization that will operate effectually among those categorically opposed to institutionalization is the problem of membership. The fact is that most twenty-first-century folk do not want, or ever intend, to "belong" to a worship group, not even to one they attend on a regular and faithful basis.[3] It is the "belonging" part that is bothersome, for traditionally that has meant intellectual assent and a more or less binding commitment. Given the Emergence predilection for loose and/or transient formation, can an ecclesial system be imagined and then sustained that operates without inherent permanence, some uniformity of assent, and responsible commitment? It is not only a good question, but it also has a kind of corollary.

A Reluctance to Belong

The reluctance to belong is an Emergence characteristic that informs all Christian bodies in this country. Predictably, it may be expected to also inform—or also afflict, as the case may be—institutional and established Christianity more and more over the coming years. Given that diminishment in sheer human and fiscal resources within inherited church, can Emergence Christian bodies pick up the slack in the maintenance of benevolent institutions and programs that have arisen out of Protestantism and been maintained by it? If not, what happens?

Given the Emergence concern about formal theology and seminaries, and given declining figures and resources within Protestantism and possibly Roman Catholicism, who will become the Christian philosophers and ethicists among us, who will train them, who will provide for their work as a community of scattered but connected scholars?

Who will be willing to let the story of our doctrines—not of our Scriptures, but of our doctrines—shape our religious imagination? Who even will know how? And given the fact that Christians, Emergence and otherwise, have usually shifted from communion to communion and from denomination to denomination with alarming ease over recent years, who, even among the most devout, will remember, much less care?[4]

Almost as central to what Emergence Christians must do or become is the fact that Christianity is no longer either socially or inherently attractive to the culture at large nor, by extension, are its symbols. Yet, as any good Jungian can demonstrate, the loss of a symbolic system and code leads directly to social and cultural disorientation, because it is in and through symbols that we human beings experience unity and transcendence.[5] Where now are the symbols that will be the salvific cohesion of a latinized Christian people? From where are those symbols to come?

There are a myriad of less heady and more practical problems wanting resolution, of course. Perhaps the most immediately pressing one is also a fairly recent arrival. Independent Emergence Christian groups and/or those which are loosely connected communions with a larger body of Christianity have not yet managed to devise a solid approach to worship and religious formation for middle-school-aged youngsters. From birth until six or seven or eight years of age, the inclusion of youngsters in adult worship or their inclusion in Emergence-style worship in a separate space and among themselves is very formative and acceptable. Likewise, inclusion of young folk over fifteen or sixteen in regular worship and study is almost a foregone conclusion. The years in between, however, are not so easily attended to.

The years between eight or nine and fifteen or sixteen are the years, in human development, where a great deal of deliberate and conscious "programming" takes place. In secular terms, they are the years where one is forced to learn the multiplication tables, long division, and basic geometry, regardless of whether or not such skills have any value in an age of calculators and cell phones. The facts of American history and government are drilled in, as are the basics of national and world geography along with a healthy hunk of basic astronomy, also to be committed to memory. A barrage of natural science is laid out for memorization, and the list goes tiresomely on and on. In sum, those are the years when we insert into children the parameters and basic tools that inform their physical world and the command of which will ensure their ability later to move easily around within it.

But those insertions require—or at least seem to require—a common agreement about what is to be programmed in, from what point of view, and toward the end of dwelling well within what ethos. They require as well a top-down imposition, or at least so far they always have. Yet both of those things are antithetical to the Emergence style and psyche. How the difficulties will be surmounted remains to be seen, but surmounted they must be.

And there are some purely emotional concerns. The "village church" or "Grandma's church where we went when I was a kid" or even "the church where we were married" is a location in physical space, but it is also a location in emotional and psychic space. It traditionally has anchored the individual, as well as serving as a point of reference for many memories and even more stories. Religion—or perhaps just religious humankind—historically has needed a place, a locus, a center. It has needed to move, body and soul, into a constructed womb made holy by the devotion and faith and prayers of hundreds and sometimes thousands of other believers. Space sometimes affirms when nothing else will.

How Emergence Christians, meeting in changing space and/or unowned and therefore transient space and/or in owned but derelict space, will compensate for this loss or shift remains to be seen. As Bishop Spong said, we are back into catacomb church, but the question of whether or not it is important to stay there is a different issue entirely.

Back to Authority

All of that also serves to bring us back again to the biggest question, the one that must be solved before any of these others has any real gravitas: Where now is the authority?

Where is the list of the authorized definitions of good and bad, right and wrong, acceptable and unacceptable? Who determines these things and then interprets them on the basis of what? Emergence society, political or otherwise, does not yet know, nor does Emergence Christianity entirely know. Yet, it seems safe to say that the latter is much nearer to an answer than is the former.

Like its predecessors in inherited church, Emergence Christianity has already asserted for itself the primacy of Scripture and of story as code. It likewise has established within every part of its machinations the primacy of community, of the body together in prayer, as agency. The question then is not so much where will authority rest and by whom will it be effected as what shall animate the union of those two and make of them a sacred authority.

It is our final question, both within these pages and far beyond them, and it has an answer—or it has the first evidences of the answer that is coming.

NOTES

1. Diana Butler Bass, "The Power of Experiential Faith," *Patheos*, September 7, 2010. Available at http://www.patheos.com/Resources/Additional-Resources/Power-of-Experiential-Faith.html.

2. Posted November 18, 2010, and http://www.emergentvillage.com/weblog/stavlund-inventive-church/.

3. For an eye-opening look at this problem, *see* Amy Frykholm, "Loose Connections: What's Happening to Church Membership?" *Christian Century*, May 31, 2011, 20–23, http://christiancentury.org/article/2011-05/loose-connections.

4. These questions have been raised often, but never more eloquently than by Martin Marty and/or Scot McKnight. *See*, in this regard, Marty's "America's Decline in Church Attendance," *Sightings*, September 26, 2010, http://divinity.uchicago.edu/martycenter/publications/sightings/archive_2010/0926.shtml; and/or McKnight's "Wiki-Stories of the Story," *Church in the Present Tense: A Candid Look at What's Emerging* (Brazos, 2011), 116f.

5. I am especially grateful to Dr. Peter Williams, a Jungian psychoanalyst, who introduced me not only to these concerns but also to the magnitude of their implications. The sustained and more complete presentation of Dr. Williams's argument is contained in *The Evolution and Transformation of Collective Symbolic Systems and the Phenomenon of "Symbolic Loss,"* an unpublished thesis submitted in completion of work toward certification as a Jungian psychoanalyst and available through Inter-Regional Society of Jungian Analysts at the Houston Jung Center, Houston, TX. See particularly pages 32f.

Afterword

All of the world's major religions are more or less identical in their morality, behavioral precepts, and social principles. It is in their mysteries that they differ. And the great mystery of Christianity is the Trinity.

That Trinity, far beyond the capacities of any grammatical language, is. It rolls and roils through human history, and It goes from thunder to glory and back again in the human heart of the believer. Its intention is the tablets in Moses's hands, the cry of Isaiah, the lament of Jeremiah, the still small voice of Elijah, the glory vision of Micah.

It came at Sinai and walked Its intention in the wilderness and across the Jordan. It ruled in David and presented to him as what could be understood—as king, mighty warrior, monarch beyond limitation.

In his progeny, It came to show Its unbreakable union with the flesh of Its making. It came as Prince to the King, as Son to the Father, as brother to the flesh; and we beheld Its majesty as of the only begotten of God.

And there were words, this time spoken without mediator. "I will ask the Father, and he will give you another Advocate, to be with you forever. This is the Spirit of Truth, whom the world cannot receive. . . . On that day you will know that I am in my Father, and you in me, and I in you. . . . I have said these things to you while I am still with you. But the Advocate, the Holy Spirit, whom the Father will send in my name will teach you everything, and remind you of all that I have said."[1]

The Trinity comes now near to the promised realization of Its intention. It comes, as It said It would. And What we saw and feared in the image of Father, What we saw and embraced as Savior-Brother, we now know as Spirit and cling to as Advocate, even as It has said of Itself from our beginning. Now, without need of image or flesh, It comes, and we receive It, as in the last of creation's ages.

This book began with a preface, and it should end, I think, with an afterword.

Whenever one speaks of anything, one speaks from a particular point of view. When one speaks of religion, one speaks from more than a point of view; one speaks from a lifetime investment in a canon or particular explication of truth. While I have tried, both in this volume and in years of lectures and other writings, to remain as objective and removed as possible from the Emergence Christianity that I have been set the task of chronicling, I know as well that I no longer enjoy the distance or objectivity that I enjoyed twenty years ago when I first began this line of study.

That said, I trust that what has been recorded in the first twenty-two chapters of this volume is as near to neutrally rendered fact and impersonal history as possible. Otherwise, my efforts in recording and yours in reading have been foiled, turned into a fool's errand, in fact, and maybe into a dangerous one at that.

When I am asked to project what the near future is for Emergence Christianity, however, then I move out of any claim of factuality or objectivity. I look, instead, whether I wish to or not, as a Christian and at what I understand to be the thrust of the story by which I have lived my life.

The words that open this chapter and precede my move into this afterword format are both mine and Emergence's. That is, they are a summation—objective and pure reportage—of what I believe to be the emerging and central core of Emergence Christianity. They are not a doctrine, though that may come. They are not a theology exactly, for they lie beyond theology and take latinized Christianity, I suspect, at last into mystery. Certainly they propose a nearer culmination to the Judeo-Christian story and, I admit, I am myself more and more persuaded by them.

Emergence Christianity is a human conversation among human conversants. It has all the limitations of that condition and will make all the mistakes and missteps patent in it. None of that will matter, I suspect, because what has happened in our lifetime seems to be more than just another semi-millennial shift. It seems instead to be more akin to the Great Transformation of two thousand years ago: less a fifth turning than a great and monumental shift.

Either way, as scholars and observers as diverse as Harvey Cox and Jürgen Moltmann have already begun to say, what comes and is already present among us is the Age of the Spirit. Where that will take us, no one, save that Spirit in Its Parts, knows. But what we, for our part, know is what our Christian forebears have always known and from the beginning have said: Blessed be God, Father, Son, and Holy Spirit, and blessed be the Trinity's holy name, now and forever more. Amen.

NOTE

1. John 14:16, 20, 25–26 NRSV.

Annotated Bibliography

All of the following titles are of importance in the broader Emergence discussion; here they have been categorized according to their particular relevance to an area of study. Books in each of the subject areas are listed in descending order according to the immediacy of their impact upon the material within that particular subsection.

Interpretive Background (Historical)

Paradise Mislaid: How We Lost Heaven . . . And How We Can Regain It, Jeffrey Burton Russell (Oxford University Press, 2006). In this brief, but tight and exquisitely researched, book, Russell manages to overview credibly and interpret brilliantly the progress of Western—i.e., Christian—thought from the Great Reformation to the current Great Emergence in which we find ourselves.

The Reformation: A History, Diarmaid MacCulloch (Viking, 2004), is a highly readable and detailed account of the events leading to and occurring within the Great Reformation. History buffs will thoroughly enjoy the style and scholarship. It is a classic on its subject.

The Great Transformation: The Beginnings of Our Religious Traditions, Karen Armstrong (Knopf, 2006). This one is a beautifully written, highly accessible overview of the Axial Age—that is, of the great social/cultural/political/economic/religious shifting that transpired in the five-plus centuries prior to the coming of Christ and that attended the rise of most of the world's great religions. A bestseller from its first day of publication, this too is a classic.

Jesus Wars: How Four Patriarchs, Three Queens, and Two Emperors Decided What Christians Would Believe for the Next 1,500 Years, Philip Jenkins (HarperOne, 2010), is as provocative as its title implies. Jenkins is a renowned scholar of ecclesio-political history, but here he outdoes even himself. The questions to which Emergence Christianity is responding and with which it is wrestling have their origins in the first half millennium of the faith, as Jenkins knows; but there could be no better explicator than he of the long way of their coming to us.

The Roads to Modernity: The British, French, and American Enlightenments, Gertrude Himmelfarb (Knopf, 2004). Not for the faint of heart, but very much for the truly curious, this book is probably the best essay popularly available on its subject. Part of the reason for that is undoubtedly that it is written by one of America's most respected moral and cultural historians.

Kepler's Witch: An Astronomer's Discovery of Cosmic Order Amid Religious War, Political Intrigue, and the Heresy Trial of His Mother, James A. Connor (HarperSanFrancisco, 2004). As jazzy and offbeat as its title, this one comes as near as any book I know of putting a very human (and immediate) face on what it meant both to be a scientist in the years of the Great Reformation and to endure the repercussions of the total upheaval that were the decades after it.

Interpretive Background (Present Day)

The Future of Faith, Harvey Cox (HarperOne, 2009). This one is Cox at his best. It is also a deliberate play, ploy, and counter to

Harris's title above. Hollis Professor of Religion Emeritus at Harvard, Cox has long stood as a giant among scholars and interpreters of religion. Arguing here that doctrine and dogma, not faith, are in decline, Cox not only takes on much of current secular humanist thought but far more significantly offers his own incisive interpretation of where religion is in this time of emergence.

The World Is Flat: A Brief History of the Twenty-First Century, Thomas Friedman (Farrar, Strauss & Giroux, 2002). Probably no book on this list needs less introduction than does this one. A bestseller almost before it was off the presses, it is far and away the most talked-about explication of the economic upheaval which is to our current era of transition as the growth of the middle class and capitalism was to the Great Reformation. A good read, it is written for the popular audience.

Wikinomics: How Mass Collaboration Changes Everything, Don Tapscott and Anthony D. Williams (Portfolio, 2008). Like several of the other books in this section, *Wikinomics* is a bestseller in the popular or general market and employs an accessible and breezy style rather than an academic one. It is, however, a very graphic presentation of the shift from modern or Industrial Age configurations in the secular marketplace to the nonhierarchal and self-organizing ones of Emergence, of why they happened, of what they look like, and of why there is no going back. Most of the insights and case studies, in other words, are easily transposed to matters of ecclesiology and institutional religion.

blink: The Power of Thinking without Thinking, Malcolm Gladwell (Little, Brown, 2005). Like Friedman's work above, *blink* hardly needs introduction. It is pertinent here only in that it exposes in very popular fashion the whole uneasiness we have about the concept of "thinking" as a proper definition of, and index for, ourselves and our beingness.

The Age of the Unthinkable: Why the New World Disorder Constantly Surprises Us and What We Can Do about It, Joshua Cooper Ramo (Little, Brown, 2009). In many ways, the subtitle of this one says it all . . . or at least lays out the parameters of the discussion. Ramo is not only a careful thinker and gifted writer but also a keen and highly insightful explicator of what is happening to us in the Great Emergence, why it is, and what we can and should do about it. In addition, he is a thinker who is filled with a considerable amount of informed hope and goodwill.

The Great Turning: From Empire to Earth Community, David C. Korten (Berrett-Koehler, 2006). Increasingly cited in discussions of the Great Emergence, this bestseller offers one of the most complete overviews of, and explanations for, the current paradigmatic shift. Korten argues that more than a five-hundred-year cycling is happening in the twenty-first century, that indeed we are witness to a complete shift in humanness and all prior forms of human structuring and governance, and that so pivotal a thing must be labeled as what it is: the Great Turning. Korten is persuasive in many of his historical interpretations, though less so in some of his applications and projections. For that reason, some of his readers may find the first four parts of the volume to be of far more pertinence than is the fifth and closing one.

Emergence: The Connected Lives of Ants, Brains, Cities, and Software, Steven Johnson (Simon & Schuster, 2001). Although it has been in circulation for several years now, this bestseller is still probably the most accessible and encompassing of popular or lay books available on Emergence Theory. It would not be a stretch to say that no one should try to grasp the changes of Emergence Christianity without first trying to comprehend the reasons behind its being called "Emergence" in the first place.

The Starfish and the Spider: The Unstoppable Power of Leaderless Organizations, Ori Brafman and Rod A. Beckstrom (Portfolio, 2006). While hardly the most weighty of studies, this one deserves our attention if, for no other reason, its own fame. On the bestseller lists for months after its 2006 release, it was *Starfish* that became the general public's first real introduction to what Emergence Theory and leaderless, nonhierarchal, self-organizing entities looked like up close and personal. It is, in other words, a rude but good-natured introduction to the realization that we have long since slipped into an Emergence modus operandi, whether we wanted to or not.

The End of Faith-Religion, Terror, and the Future of Reason, Sam Harris (Norton, 2004). Harris, because of his work in neuroscience, is perhaps the most articulate and accessible of the activists within the secular humanist movement or sensibility. While devout believers of any organized faith will find his arguments inflammatory at worst and distressing at least, his line of reasoning needs to be read and dissected by those who wish to understand with any kind of completeness the nature of our current cultural and social discussions as well as our rising secularization.

Interpretive Commentary on Current Christianity

Witness to Dispossession: The Vocation of a Post-Modern Theologian, Tom Beaudoin (Orbis, 2008). Beaudoin, an associate professor of practical theology at Fordham University's Graduate School of Religion, is regarded as one of the most influential and powerful theologians working in this country and abroad. While his work is not for the faint of heart, it is central to the fullest understanding of Emergence Christianity—its theology, its context, and its thrust. Those who venture here will be richly rewarded.

The Practicing Congregation: Imagining a New Old Church and/or *From Nomads to Pilgrims: Stories from Practicing*

Congregations, Diana Butler Bass (The Alban Institute, 2004 and 2006 respectively, with Joseph Stewart-Sicking as coauthor on the second). Bass is the recognized Anglican authority on the current evolution of re-traditioning mainline churches. Her work is being used all over the country as a diagnostic tool for parishes and dioceses. To approach the response to Emergent Church by mainline Protestantism without her insights would be not only foolhardy but almost impossible.

Paradoxy: Creating Christian Community beyond Us and Them, Ken Howard (Paraclete Press, 2010). With a foreword by Brian McLaren and an afterword by Paul Zahl, this one has all the bona fides any book could want, and both of them are richly deserved. Howard offers both a sharp-eyed analysis of how the church has arrived at its present permutation, followed by a very accessible and kindly intended diagnosis of what its condition presently is. More importantly, perhaps, Howard gives us one of the clearest and most concise commentaries presently available about where the church may reasonably be seen as going in this time of paradigmatic shift. Additionally, each chapter concludes with some penetrating questions about the implications of what has just been presented, a boon not only to individual readers but also to leaders of small groups.

The Phoenix Affirmations, Eric Elnes (Jossey-Bass, 2006). This volume was, and remains, a kind of "Here I Stand" declaration for that part of mainline Christianity that, under the banner of Progressive Christianity, is hesitating between re-traditioning or reconfiguring into the new Protestantism and/or becoming fully Emergent.

Elnes, a UCC pastor in Omaha, Nebraska, is a brilliant observer of the intersection between culture and faith (google Darkwood Brew or *see* www.crosswalkamerica.org to understand the full implications of what he is daring) and a clear-eyed student of the theological shifts involved in our current and heated ecclesial discussions.

An Emerging Theology for Emerging Churches, Ray S. Anderson (InterVarsity, 2006). Anderson's development of the idea that the relationship between Jerusalem (inherited church) and Antioch (or fresh expression of church) was almost identical to the current unease and distress between established denominations and Emergence Christianity is brilliant. It is also quite clear in the obligations it lays on both sides of the aisle to understand the implications and responsibilities of being Christian—together, but different—within the confines of one time period. Last of all, it is remarkably liberating for many readers to discover that the church has been here before and quite probably will be here again.

The Hidden Power of Electronic Culture: How Media Shapes Faith, the Gospel, and Church, Shane Hipps (Zondervan, 2005). This deceptively easygoing book deftly weaves Marshall McLuhan and Co. into an at-times brilliantly insightful critique of current "church." It's well worth the time it takes to read it and more than worth the time it takes to ponder it.

Spirit and Flesh: Life in a Fundamentalist Baptist Church, James M. Ault Jr. (Knopf, 2004). Ault has produced one of the most poignant but clear-eyed studies to date of the "fundamental fundamentalist" community. Humane and human in its approach and appeal, this record of time among people whom he came to hold in affection as well as despair should be required reading for every liberal Christian who thinks one side of the current conversation is admirable and the other totally without redemptive virtue.

The Post-Evangelical, Dave Tomlinson (UK edition, SPCK, 1995; US edition, YS Specialties, 2003). The first volume to deal head-on and clearly with the disintegration of evangelicalism, *Post* was, and remains as, a groundbreaking and insightful presentation of what evangelicalism was becoming in response to post-modernism. Perhaps just as much to the point is the fact that the book was, and continues to be, of great pastoral importance and guidance to many evangelicals who have found themselves trapped firmly in what has been, but yet without any working knowledge of how either to understand what was happening to them or to escape from it into a renewed and more generous exercise of the faith.

The New Faces of Christianity: Believing the Bible in the Global South and/or *The Next Christendom: The Coming of Global Christianity*, Philip Jenkins (Oxford University Press, 2002 and 2006 respectively). Jenkins, Distinguished Professor of History and Religious Studies at Penn State, is perhaps our most-trusted and most-quoted authority on the subject of globalizing Christianity. Readers will find his take on globalization's impact on first world Christianity's present situation, as well as on our immediate future, to be immensely helpful and immensely unsettling. Jenkins has another work forthcoming in September 2012 which promises to be even more revelatory of patterns, especially for communions that have international reach and concerns.

Those who do not have time to read the above volumes themselves will find Jenkins's work readily accessible in precis on the web from sources like *The Atlantic Monthly*. Even a passing familiarity with what he is telling us about our world will be of benefit.

Rising from the Ashes: Rethinking Church, Becky Garrison (Seabury Books, 2007). Garrison is an editor with the *Wittenburg Door* and is by profession a religion satirist. She is also more knowledgeable about Emergence Christianity than almost any other reporter covering the print media scene. In *Rising*, and in her 2009 companion release, *Jesus Died for This?*, Garrison has managed to present with biting clarity many of the major voices and issues that are shaping North American Christianity in the twenty-first century.

The Next Evangelicalism: Freeing the Church from Western Cultural Captivity, Soong-Chan Rah (InterVarsity, 2009). Soong-Chan Rah is Milton B. Engebretson Assistant Professor of Church Growth and Evangelism at North Park University as well as first-generation American. He speaks with brilliance as well as from a strong base of both academic and personal knowledge about the interplay between latinized and non-latinized Christianity as Emergence Christianity is forming. Like Jenkins, who enthusiastically endorses his work, Soong-Chan sees a global Christianity that is stripped of its latinized heritage and reshaped into something very different from previous expressions of the faith.

An Introduction to the Theology of Religions: Biblical, Historical, and Contemporary Perspectives, Veli-Matti Karkkainen (InterVarsity, 2003). The theology of religion—i.e., of how we can live with integrity as faithful adherents to one faith in a world of many faiths—is one of the two most compelling issues facing the next quarter to half century of Christian thinking; and Professor Karkkainen is one of our leading thinkers and commentators on the subject. This book, while it is probably most appropriately addressed now by those with considerable interest in the subject, is still worthy of mention here; for awareness of Karkkainen's work will be requisite very soon for any serious discussion of the issues involved.

Who's Afraid of Post-Modernism: Taking Derrida, Lyotard, and Foucault to Church, James K. A. Smith (Baker Academic, 2006). For those who want to get a concise, albeit evangelical and radical, distillation of what postmodernism is and what it means to at least some large part of the American church, this book is a godsend. It is short, authoritatively presented, and accessible.

The Next Reformation: Why Evangelicals Must Embrace Postmodernity, Carl Raschke (Baker Academic, 2004). Like Smith's *Who's Afraid*, this book comes from an evangelical perspective, but it is a superb analysis of what is happening to us currently, just as it is a useful engagement of the emerging new body of Christianity.

The Great Worship Awakening: Singing a New Song in the Post-Modern Church, Robb Redman (Jossey-Bass, 2002). Redman, a Presbyterian pastor in San Antonio, is a vice president of Maranatha! Music and, as a result, intimately involved in the changing landscape of American worship—its whys and wherefores, its implications, and its influence on the Emerging Church movement. A gentle read, this book is also an informative one for seeing the world outside of ECUSA *and* for understanding why the community church that blends Anglican liturgy with postmodern worship is not a hodgepodge or an offense but rather an almost inevitable next step for many Christians in this culture.

A New Spiritual Home: Progressive Christianity at the Grass Roots, Hal Taussig (Polebridge Press, 2006). A Methodist pastor and Visiting Professor at Union Theological, Taussig has also been associated with the Westar Institute and the fellows of the Jesus Seminar. He brings to this overview of contemporary American Christendom a liberal, but still very pastoral and professorial interpretation of where Christian theology really is in the minds of many pew-dwellers and former pew-dwellers.

Core Texts from and about Emergence Christianity

A Generous Orthodoxy, Brian McLaren (Zondervan, 2004). While this title has a subtitle, even a casual glance at its cover will tell you why the whole is not included here. McLaren is the acknowledged leader of Emergence Christianity, the Martin Luther of our current reformation. Any reader over twenty (and some who are younger) will find much to deplore here and much to applaud. Either way, one should think of this volume as being a kind of contemporary edition of the Ninety-Five Theses tacked to the door of the church in Wittenberg five centuries ago.

A New Kind of Christianity: Ten Questions That Are Transforming the Faith, Brian McLaren (HarperOne, 2010). *A New Kind* is an expression, richer and fully mature six years later, of the concepts underlying *A Generous Orthodoxy*. It is also, theologically speaking, "the shot heard 'round the world," for no other contemporary book in Christian theology has so stirred the interest, and enlivened the conversation, about Emergence Christianity as has this one. It would be essentially impossible, in fact, to understand how and why the battle lines are being drawn both within Emergence and among the other major communions of faith without at some point reading what McLaren is saying here.

mission-shaped church: Church Planting and Fresh Expressions of Church in a Changing Context, the Church of England's Mission and Public Affairs Council (Church House Publishing, 2004). Despite its having been in print for some half-dozen years or so, this is still the most useful, informing, and practical text presently available both for understanding what fresh expressions of church are and of how to go about the business of enabling them. Available in hardcopy from the usual sources, it is also available for download and itself includes a considerable number of websites of great pertinence to the matter at hand.

Over the years since its initial release in 2004, *mission-shaped* has become so influential and significant as to spawn, in 2010, a miniseries of related titles, each of them a strong contributor to the overarching discussion of mission-shaped church: *Mission-Shaped Questions*, + Steven Croft, ed.; *Mission-Shaped Parish: Traditional Church in a Changing World*, Paul Bayes et al.; and *Mission-Shaped Spirituality*, Susan Hope. All are published in the United States by Seabury Books, an imprint of the Church Publishing Group.

A Christianity Worth Believing, Doug Pagitt (Jossey-Bass, pbk. 2009). This very lively, candid, and accessible book gives voice and body to the basic theology of the Great Emergence in a way that most previous essays have failed to do. It also enjoys a subtitle that's worth looking up just for the joy of reading it . . . and the book is even better.

The Fidelity of Betrayal: Towards a Church beyond Belief, Peter Rollins (Paraclete Press, 2008), and *How [Not] to Speak of God* (also Paraclete Press, 2008). Rollins, the founder of Ikon in Ireland, is a leader internationally in the Emergence movement. He also holds a PhD in philosophy. The two together make him singularly well-equipped to be one of the outstanding thinkers and theologians of the twenty-first century. He is especially brilliant and accessible in these two volumes.

Emerging Churches: Creating Christian Community in Postmodern Cultures, Eddie Gibbs and Ryan K. Bolger (Baker Academic, 2005). I keep this one on my desktop for ready reference. Those who want a field guide to the Emergent movement will find it invaluable. Its lists of the churches now within this movement, its precise presentation of how mainline churches are church-planting within the emergent movement, and its brief bios of the major players make this one worth a long look.

The New Christians: Dispatches from the Emergent Frontier, Tony Jones (Jossey-Bass, 2008). Jones, who has been intimately involved in Emergent Christianity and in Emergent Village from its inception, is a brilliant apologist for Emergent theology and sensibilities. He is also an accessible and brilliant explicator of all these things. Every student of Emergent thought should read this one carefully.

Sin: A History, Gary A. Anderson (Yale, 2009). Atonement and a defensible doctrine about it—or understanding of it—are central to Emergence work. In full knowledge of that fact and of the impenetrable forest of words and theories that have encrusted atonement since the days of Second Temple Judaism, Anderson here offers up a startling interpretation of the evolution of Judeo-Christian conceptualizations of sin and, by extension, of atonement.

Jesus, Paul and the People of God: A Theological Dialogue with N. T. Wright, Nicholas Perrin and Richard B. Hays, eds. (IVP Academic, 2011). Wright's importance to the Emergence Christian conversation cannot be overestimated, especially as it affects and informs the more evangelical thinkers and leaders within Emergence. Again, the book is not for the faint of heart, but there could be no better window into Wright's Emergence theology and/or into the more evangelically inclined thinker's engagement of it than this collection of essays. The serious student of what is happening in today's Christian conversation will find this one as rewarding as it is illuminating.

Church in the Present Tense: A Candid Look at What's Emerging, Kevin Corcoran, ed. (Brazos Press, 2011). Corcoran edits his offerings and those of three other theologians, philosophers, and spiritual scholars from both America and England who are steeped in Emergence Christianity. Those looking for theory, core theology, and/or intellectual heft dealing with Emergence in today's culture will find it here.

An Emergent Manifesto of Hope, Doug Pagitt and Tony Jones, eds. (Baker, 2007). This is a candid, thorough, and dynamic collection of essays by some two dozen leaders of the Great Emergence. Anyone even mildly curious about what Emergent and the next Christianity are will be well served by three or four hours with these men and women . . . not to mention being deeply assured and affirmed by the passion of their faith and vocation even as they give to the church a new face and a new way of doing its business.

Naked Spirituality: A Life with God in Twelve Simple Words, Brian McLaren (Hodder & Stoughton, 2011). The temptation with this volume is to add a whole new category to this annotated bibliography, because yet once again, McLaren has broken new ground. In this volume, he opens up the whole pastoral area of "counseling on personal practices for individual Emergence Christians." In using his own history as well as general commentary, McLaren goes outside and beyond the fundamentalist roots of his youth and hits the center of Emergence spiritual quest. While as a reader, one will find here very little new ground for spirituality per se, he or she will witness Emergence making tradition palatable by disconnecting it from religiosity.

Free for All: Rediscovering the Bible in Community, Tim Conder and Daniel Rhodes (Baker, 2009). Conder is founding pastor and Rhodes is co-pastor of Emmaus Way in Durham, North Carolina, one of the United States's better-known missional or Emergence bodies. Among the questions pressing upon Emergence theologians and Christians currently is that of the authority of Scripture and of how best to understand and define it. In this very clear and careful volume, Conder and Rhodes offer an approach that is consonant with Emergence thought while also being respectful of the fact that a theology of Scripture is still a work in process for most post-Reformation Christians.

Bonhoeffer: Pastor, Martyr, Prophet, Spy, Eric Metaxas (Thomas Nelson, 2010), is a delightfully rendered and richly informative lay, rather than academic, study of the life and thoughts of one of the twentieth century's great thinkers and Christian theologians. Bonhoeffer's continuing effect on Emergence thought can not be overstated; and this accessible, but thorough précis of his work offers invaluable insights into the nature and content of the Bonhoeffer legacy.

Emerging and Fresh Expressions of Church: How Are They Authentically Church and Anglican?, Ian J. Mobsby (Moot Community Publishing, 2007). The tendency among North American Christians often is to see Emergent and Emerging Christianity as an American experience of American origin. In actuality,

Emergence was far more discernible in the United Kingdom in the last decades of the twentieth century than it was in the United States. Mobsby's slim volume, while not always easy reading for Americans, is nonetheless a classic in its overview of Emergence in England and in its singular accommodations with Anglicanism, making this a useful study for all who are interested in the new Christianity both in terms of the established branches of Protestantism and in terms of international patterns.

Ancient Faith, Future Mission: Fresh Expressions in the Sacramental Tradition, Steven Croft and Ian Mobsby, eds. (Canterbury Press, 2009). The first volume in the Ancient Faith, Future Mission series, this collection of essays by sixteen leaders and students of Emergence Christianity on both sides of the pond is a hearty and muscular introduction to how it's done, why it's done, and by whom it's done, "it" being Emergence worship in many, if not most, of its presenting forms and configurations. This one is a delightful read, as well as an informing one.

Published in the United States as *Ancient Faith, Future Mission: Fresh Expressions in the Sacramental Tradition*, Steven Croft, Ian Mobsby, and Stephanie Spellers, eds. (Seabury Books, 2010).

Everything Must Change: When the World's Biggest Problems and Jesus' Good News Collide, Brian McLaren (Nelson, 2007). While hardly light reading, this fairly recent statement from McLaren is nonetheless the clearest and most energized exposition to date of the radical world vision of the Emergent movement in this country.

Lesslie Newbigin: Missionary Theologian: A Reader, compiled and introduced by Paul Weston (Eerdmans, 2006). While a good dozen or so of the twentieth-century's theologians and thinkers have had a lasting and powerful impact on Emergence Christianity, none has left quite so signatory a heritage as has Newbigin. A large part of Emergence Christianity—indeed, many would argue the larger part, worldwide—defines and names itself as "missional Christianity" or "missional church." Those who do so find their roots and basic tenets in Newbigin. For that reason, any serious student of Emergence Christianity needs to be at least passingly familiar with Newbigin's work; and Weston has done a superb job of distilling his work into an accessible and surprisingly thorough précis for us.

Signs of Emergence: A Vision for Church That Is Organic/Networked/Decentralized/Bottom-up/Communal/Flexible {Always Evolving}, Kester Brewin (Baker, 2007). Unfortunately, the complete impact of Brewin's subtitle cannot be conveyed without more visual design than is feasible here, though the above is an attempt at suggesting some of the possibilities explored there. Brewin, a Londoner, is one of the founding leaders of Vaux, an alternative worship group in the city. He is also a fine storyteller and recorder of what Emergence is in real life among real people. This book has been very influential in both this country and the United Kingdom.

The Hyphenateds: How Emergence Christianity Is Re-Traditioning Mainline Practices, Phil Snider, ed. (Chalice Press, 2011). This energetic collection of essays by Hyphenated leaders from across several natal denominational lines is probably the best window presently available anywhere into both what a Hyphenated is in relation to other parts of Emergence Christianity and also into what the Hyphenateds' role as "re-traditioners" already is and may grow to become.

Simply Christian: *Why Christianity Makes Sense* (HarperSanFrancisco, 2006) and *Surprised by Hope* (HarperOne, 2008), both by N. T. Wright, the bishop of Durham. These two books will, I suspect, stand for decades as classics in Christian apology. Together, they certainly constitute the best in the theology of Emerging Christianity.

Some parts of Wright's theology will offend American Christians; hopefully, most of it will not. Rather, they will find here a reasoned and pastoral voice offering a blessed place of thoughtful and faithful quiet in the midst of an otherwise disturbing storm system. Well worth the read by folk on all sides of our current debates, the first is the kind of "lest we forget" book that's good for all of us now and again; and the second is a clarion call to a reconsidered Christian theology.

After Our Likeness: The Church as the Image of the Trinity, Miroslav Volf (Eerdmans, 1998). Few theologians working today have had a more pervasive and sustained influence on Emergence theology and ecclesiology than has Volf. Likewise, probably none of his very influential books has had any greater impact than has this one, particularly in the area of ecclesiology. Many Emergence leaders openly claim it as a "must read" for any Emergence theologian or theorist.

Sun of Righteousness, ARISE!: God's Future for Humanity and the Earth, Jürgen Moltmann (Fortress Press, 2010). Emergence theology draws heavily from mid- to late-twentieth-century thinkers like Rahner, Newbigin, and Bonhoeffer, but perhaps no theologian from that chronological grouping has been more influential and seminal for Emergence than has Moltmann, who, now in his eighties, continues to work as insightfully and brilliantly as ever. In this, his most recent title, he takes on a panoply of ideas and concepts that, he argues, obstruct today's Christian from fully comprehending the actuality of the kingdom of God here and now and always.

The Becoming of G-d: What the Trinitarian Nature of God Has to Do with Church and a Deep Spirtuality for the Twenty-First Century, Ian Mobsby (YTC Press, 2008). Mobsby, who is pastor at Moot and a priest in the Church of England, is one of the most widely recognized leaders in Emergence both in the United Kingdom and internationally. In this small volume, however, he shines as a practical theologian. Emergence Christianity is profoundly trinitarian, and Mobsby does a superb job of explicating exactly what that means and what it translates to on the ground.

The Wisdom of Stability: Rooting Faith in a Mobile Culture, Jonathan Wilson-Hartgrove (Paraclete Press, 2010). Neo-monasticism is one of the principal segments as well as principal attributes and characteristics of Emergence Christianity; and Wilson-Hartgrove is a principal leader and explicator of it in both the United States and abroad. In this delightful and low-key book, he makes his case with simplicity, but, paradoxically, he also makes it powerfully. *Wisdom* is a beautiful book that not only presents the specifics of Wilson-Hartgrove's own community but also presents as well much of the Emergence theology underlying Neo-monasticism itself.

The New Conspirators: Creating the Future One Mustard Seed at a Time, Tom Sine (InterVarsity, 2008). Sine, a founder along with his wife, Christine, of the Mustard Seed Community, is an expert on Neo-monasticism and its placement within Emergence Christianity. His overview here will be invaluable to those trying to understand what this renewed and radical ancient sensibility is about in today's world.

Informing Texts about Virtual Church and Emergence Christianity

Church in the Inventive Age, Doug Pagitt (Sparkhouse, 2010). This one is the sleekest, no-nonsense, just-the-facts-Jack manual on the market for those who want to engage in practice, as well as understanding, just what "church" can and must do in a digital age. Pagitt, a major leader in Emergent Church, delivers an information-loaded bonanza for contemporary Christianity, whether it be Emergence or not.

SimChurch: Being Church in the Virtual World, Douglas Estes (Zondervan, 2009). Estes, who is adjunct professor of the New Testament at Western Seminary in San Jose as well as lead pastor at Berryessa Valley Church in San Jose, offers the most even-handed, informed, and insightful overview to date of what virtual world ecclesia means not only within its own confines but also to ecclesia in the physical world. At the risk of overstating the case, it is increasingly incumbent upon clergy and lay leaders alike to familiarize themselves now . . . right now . . . with the material Estes renders so clearly.

Tweet If You ❤ Jesus: Practicing Church in the Digital Reformation, Elizabeth Drescher (Morehouse Publishing, 2011). Drescher, a brilliant columnist who also teaches at the University of California Santa Clara, here provides the most insightful analysis to date of what digitalization means both to the faith itself and also to the institutions it has erected. Far beyond the much-discussed implications of social media and even farther beyond the ephemeral tweet and twitter of its visually clever titling, this volume lays bare what it means to be alive and responsible within Reformation.

The Hidden Power of Electronic Culture: How Media Shapes Faith, the Gospel, and Church, Shane Hipps (Zondervan, 2005). This deceptively easygoing book deftly weaves Marshall McLuahn and Co. into an at-times brilliantly insightful critique of current "church." It's well worth the time it takes to read it and more than worth the time to ponder it.

Index

PHYLLIS TICKLE is the founding editor of the Religion Department of *Publishers Weekly* and an authority on religion in America. A former academic and college dean, Tickle is the author of some two dozen books on the subject including, most recently, the best-selling volume, *The Great Emergence: How Christianity Is Changing and Why* and *The Words of Jesus: A Gospel of the Sayings of Our Lord*. She makes her home with her physician husband on a small farm in rural West Tennessee.